IN SEARCH OF THE PINK FLAMINGO

DITCH THE EXPECTATIONS OF OTHERS, OWN YOUR VOICE, AND BE YOUR UNUSUAL SELF

CHANEL ROBE

WINNERS PRESS

Published in the United States by Winners Press, an imprint of Winners LLC, winnerspress.com.

ISBN: 979-8-9877517-1-8

Printed in the United States of America

CONTENTS

Introduction   v

PART I
1. Church Lies   3
2. Game of Pretense   15
3. My Wide Empty Smile   27
4. Close, but Not Closer   37

PART II
5. The Journey Starts with A Sneaky God   47
6. In Search of Strongholds   67
7. Separating Playmates   79
8. Subdued Emotions and Surface Relationships   91
9. The Me God Sees   103

PART III
10. Flamingo Pink   121
11. Next Step: Put This Into Practice   141

Notes   143
Acknowledgments   145
About the Author   147

INTRODUCTION

I felt the headphones I had fallen asleep with steadily drawn behind me. Half asleep, I turned onto my right side to find that a man had somehow gotten into my bedroom. Shrouded by the darkness of the early morning, he knelt at my bedside. When he noticed that I was awake, he dove for my throat. As I tried to scream, his thick hands wrapped tightly around my slender neck and squeezed tightly.

"No!"

I shot awake with a yell. My fingers clutched my neck as I frantically searched every corner of my dimly lit bedroom. *It was just a nightmare! It was just a nightmare!* I desperately tried to calm my racing heart. *It was just a nightmare!* But it felt so real.

"The enemy is trying to steal your voice," the Holy Spirit whispered.

That was not the first or the last time the enemy would try to kill, steal, and destroy my voice, the very thing that the Lord had purposed for me to use to do His work.

My voice, in this case, was not just my ability to speak; it was how I showed up daily. It was who I showed up as daily. At the time, I did not realize that the enemy's deceptions and schemes ran deeper than I could have ever imagined. I thought I had stopped his efforts and was owning my voice, but the truth was that the horse was already out the gate in many areas of my life.

Although I looked like I had it all together, when you examined my life, a different picture emerged. I was struggling. I struggled to fit in and live up to the weighty daily expectations of being a Christian, daughter, sister and professional. I had surface relationships with myself, God, family, and friends; I struggled with secret sins that left me riddled with shame and guilt. My true self sat on the backbench of my life and screamed for a chance to be seen and heard, but I was afraid and unsure how to let her out without being judged.

But God was faithful enough not to leave me in the state I was in. There was purpose assigned to every part of my voice, way beyond anything I could even imagine. I was barely scratching the surface and needed to reclaim the pieces the devil had stolen so that I was free from the expectations of others and empowered to own my voice.

As I reclaimed those pieces one step at a time, I felt led to share parts of my story with others around me, and a pattern emerged. Many were shocked at what I had gone through, and even more raised their hand to admit that they were struggling too and needed help. I realized that my voice was needed far beyond what I could imagine, so I decided to share my story.

My journey to owning my voice will empower you to own your voice. You will know that you were never meant to suffer in silence or feel alone. I'm taking the first step to share so that you are encouraged by the knowledge that we all struggle with thorns in our flesh and the fruits of trauma, even as Christians walking daily with Christ. You *can* walk in freedom and become a sin-overcoming, trauma-conquering, generational-curse breaker as you experience breakthroughs from the secret sins and traumas that held you and your family captive for generations.

This book will show you that you can ditch the weight of continuously struggling and striving for perfection because God's plan for you is built on progression, not perfection or good works.

You will learn strategies and practical tips to ditch the daily façade and open the door of your heart and show God your true feelings and daily struggles. As I share my heart with you, be inspired by the awareness that you too can have deeper intimate relationships and be real with yourself, Christ, and others. You can be freed from the expectations of others and own your voice fully so you can have the life and impact that God has purposed for you.

Those may seem like lofty goals, but I'm confident in what God can accomplish through my voice. So, fasten your seatbelt and let me take you on a journey. It all started with a moment when I nearly lost something I valued above all else.

PART I

Look at me
You may think you see
Who I really am
But you'll never know me.

– Christina Aguilera

1

CHURCH LIES

"God, please don't let me die this way. I'm too young!"

Moments earlier, I was fast asleep, lost in a dream where Louis Armstrong's gravelly baritone provided the musical score. The lyrics soothed me and coaxed my lips into a lazy smile. *Then I think to myself, what a wonderful world.*

Suddenly, everything went pitch black except for the constantly moving black-and-white spiral pattern before my eyes. Disoriented by the change, I stared wide-eyed, more petrified than a deer stuck in the glare of the headlights of an oncoming car. *What is going on?*

Before I could make sense of what was in front of me, an unseen force swiftly sucked my entire body, feet-first, into the epicentre of the spiralling circles. An invisible hand changed the channel, and there on the screen was a scene from an afternoon four weeks earlier in vivid colour. I raised my hands instinctively to the sides of my head. I needed to touch something real and protect my memories from being kidnapped and broadcast on the screen, but the motion was interrupted by another abrupt channel change.

The swirling, spiralling circles reappeared, and I screamed hysterically.

"Somebody, help me!"

I was sucked screaming into the abyss of spiralling black and white. My arms flailed wildly as I tumbled free-fall down the tunnel-like gyrating hole.

I was startled out of sleep with a gurgled yell, my chest heaving as I gasped for air. Blind panic infused every bead of sweat that washed over me. A new scene was hijacked from my memories and cast onto the screen. *But I'm awake now, aren't I? How is this happening?* I was in a stupor, a twilight between dream and reality, and my mind raced to deduce the meaning.

It was the oddest thing. My eyes darted around my bedroom to confirm that I was wide awake. Yet, my mind played a scene from my past as though I was a character on a TV screen.

I moved to swing my legs off the bed, but nothing happened. I was paralysed. I opened my mouth to scream for help, but it froze, muted like a frightening pantomime. I felt caged inside my own body but stubbornly willed my hand to move. It worked. Inside, I sobbed with joy, but something was still very wrong. My hand movement was disjointed and robotic, swift and rigid.

Then, as if enlivened by a force not my own, my body slung itself off the bed and lurched into the ensuite bathroom.

I found myself pressed against the cold outer wall that stood between my body and a two-storey drop of open space on the other side of my second-floor apartment. Whatever had taken control of me tried repeatedly to pull me through the wall to my death two floors below.

"God, please, please! Don't let me die! I'm too young to die!"

I pleaded pitifully, but God did not seem to be listening. Instead, the swirling circles continued. I was wide awake, but my mind was trapped in another dimension, seemingly disembodied, spiralling into another black-and-white circular tunnel. I was free-falling into a bottomless chasm pausing only to abruptly land in another time slice from two weeks ago. As I struggled in vain to regain control of my twenty-five-year-old self, I had an earth-shattering revelation – I had lost the thing I valued the most, *my mind and the control it gave me*. I was altered, turned inside out, but this was not the end of me. It was an unholy graduation ceremony for an awakening that had started years before.

Curiosity killed the cat, they say. Well, it did and didn't for me. I got baptised when I was fourteen, not because Christ had won my heart or I was sorry for anything I had done in the past. Nope, not this girl. I got baptised because I was curious.

A few weeks before my big day, my friend had gotten baptised and soon received the Holy Spirit. Seeing her get overwhelmed by this invisible presence was intriguing and beautiful. I stood transfixed, watching as her hands flung backwards and her body arched as a shrill "Hallelujah!" erupted from her lips. She sounded nothing like the calm, follow-the-rules girl I knew. And then something amazing happened. Unearthly sounds bubbled up from inside her, and an ecstatic language like I'd never heard flowed from her mouth. It sounded like Chinese.

To say the occurrence piqued my curiosity was the understatement of the century. Like a moth drawn to the proverbial dancing flames, I decided whatever it was she had, I wanted it. So, almost as casually as a child picking her favourite candy at the candy store without a care in the world or consideration of the cost, I took the cold plunge. Moments later, I emerged like a shiny new coin, dressed in a dripping wet white gown and a stranger's misfit underwear. I made what many told me would be a life-changing decision all on my own, without the consent of my mother, who, after hearing the "good news," immediately declared, "She is not ready!"

She was right. A few weeks later, I confessed to my friend.

"I'm not a Christian yet."

Her brows knitted. I could literally see the wheels churning in her head as a confused "What do you mean? Aren't you baptised?" sprung from her lips. My statement certainly perplexed her, but it was the truest I would be to myself and others for the next few years.

She assumed that being dunked in the baptismal pool made me a Christian, but all it did was make me soaking wet, and I felt anything but Christian-like. I tried to explain as best as a fourteen-year-old could that my heart wasn't yet transformed. Going down in the water to me was almost like taking a dip at my favourite beach on a chilly day. It was a moment that meant very little to me. It wasn't life-changing after all, and I didn't even consider it memorable enough to record my baptismal date.

While my baptism meant little beyond a curious escapade to me, I unknowingly entered a new arena that called for something I wasn't ready for or prepared to give – religious perfection. I was the circle, and the church was the square. We didn't fit. I felt stifled and forced to put on an act of being at a place spiritually that I did not even know was on the map. *Fake it 'til you make it* was the order of the day.

You see, I had gotten baptised in the Apostolic church. As a member, I was expected to look the part. That meant swapping out my pants for long skirts and dresses, wearing church-approved hats, and sacrificing wearing jewellery and dreaming aloud of the day I would grow up, leave my mother's house, and pierce my ears.

In the early days of my pseudo-conversion, I held onto my worldly ways for as long as I could get away with it. I kept wearing my pants and would sneak past the church to catch my bus hoping nobody saw me. Three months into it, my heart decided that it had had enough of the pressure and worry of being caught and made an honest Christian girl out of me, at least on the surface. I packed every single pair of my dearly beloved pants into a black plastic shopping bag with the solemnity of a funeral service and told my mom to give them away, burying them once and for all in someone else's wardrobe. Mission 1 accomplished.

At the time, I only had two skirts that I wore constantly until my mother could afford to buy me more. Nonetheless, my exterior refurbishing was done, complete with the trimmings of a well-learned and perfectly-timed "I'm blessed and highly favoured" greeting and a fancy-dancy church hat.

I was the old house that looked bright and appealing on the outside, but under the fresh coat of paint, it was cracked, chipped and peeling. Inside I was decrepit and run-down with mice playing tag all day long across my red-stained, dilapidated wooden floors. I desperately needed a thorough spring cleaning of the heart, but no one noticed. I had the shiny exterior of a Christian church girl, but inside, the me they could not see was running things, and boy, did she have fun luring me down the enticing path to taste forbidden fruits.

One year, a juicy scandal happened at my huge but conservative church. A lead-singer choir member got pregnant for a well-respected brother. It took one whisper of the situation for the news to spread like wildfire long before the consequence of their entanglement was visible. Typical to a lot of religious settings, the woman bore the brunt of the blame. The poor sister couldn't show her face in the congregation because everyone knew, and the religious vultures swooped down on their prey, picking her to bits for being, in their opinion, so weak and foolish as to let something like that happen. Lesson learned: when you "sin big" – so everybody can see what you've done – you pay big religious fines. I resolved that if I ever messed up – big or small – I would never, ever let anybody find out.

The same year I was baptised, I was born again in another unexpected way. I had my first orgasm. My initiation into reading romance novels started with what I call a "small sin." At twelve years old, I disobeyed a direct command to leave a certain set of books alone and chose to feed my voracious reading appetite with a beguiling new forbidden fruit. Reading them was quite filling and strangely exciting.

I did not understand many of the sexual scenes that I read about. Then one day, my brain keyed in to the unrelenting tingling sensation I felt between my legs whenever I read a particularly steamy scene. It made me blush and glance around furtively to check if anyone was watching. After weeks of feeding my ever-growing appetite and unyielding curiosity, I finally rubbed the source of the insistent sensations and heeded the unfamiliar but relentless urge to persist until I experienced the momentary rapture of unexpected release.

The feeling left a lingering impression that made me eager to experience it again and again. And with that, I walked into the prison cell of my own lust and willingly handed over the keys. Masturbation became my cellmate with no chance of parole. That's when my double-agent religious life escalated to another level.

As my new jailor enticed and groomed me to its lascivious hands, my religious duties grew. I became more involved in church-related activities. I felt like I was being pulled in three different directions. There was a constant struggle between who God wanted me to be, who the church said I should be, and what my body was dictating I should be. None of them agreed. All three battled for possession of my soul, mind, will and emotions, and whoever won control of the soul automatically ruled my body.

When I was fifteen, the moment I had so fiercely coveted after watching my friend's spiritual encounter a year before was granted. Standing at the front of the church while everyone sang praises to God, an image unlike any other filled my mind's eye. I suddenly saw, in vivid detail, Jesus on His cross. The bloody wounds etched by whips onto His back were on full display; His body was a mangled mass of flesh, blood, and gravelly dirt. I looked with horror and awe at where the crown of thorns pierced deeply into His disfigured head with excruciating pain too horrific to bear. I looked at His hands ripped by the large rusty nails that kept Him fastened onto the roughly cut timber. My lips trembled, and my closed eyes unleashed tears that exploded uncontrollably until there wasn't one dry corner left, inside or out. The realisation of His sacrifice hit me like never before. He did all this for me!

I was a sight! My usual calm, follow-the-rules self was doubled over, completely oblivious to how I looked or sounded to anyone else. Then, in between broken sobs, unearthly sounds bubbled up from inside me, and an ecstatic language unlike anything I had ever heard flowed from my mouth. The Holy Spirit – the manifestation of God who stays with us – had taken over my entire being. It was the evidence my church needed. He now lived in me, but sadly, I relegated Him to that part of my life that only showed up on Sundays.

I would have been a strong contender for the Emmy Award for Best Christian Actress had there been such a category. To many, I was a promising youth leader who had the potential to become a heavy-hitting teacher and prophetess in the Apostolic church, but only God and I knew the truth. Sundays from 08:30

a.m. to 08:30 p.m. were the only times I held sacred and resisted the desire to meet up with my cellmate – most of the time. I was a spiritually bankrupt fraud and a functioning Christian masturbation addict.

I was out of control. Lust had completely taken over, and sexual thoughts invaded my mind demanding immediate satisfaction. When I didn't get my masturbation fix, I became distracted, antsy, and downright irritable. I had created a habit, and now my habit was creating me.

As my addiction grew, the romance novels weren't stimulating enough anymore. I needed something stronger. Erotica became my drug of choice. I always needed a new piece to get my next release, even if I had to steal or borrow a physical or virtual copy of a much-desired book. My favourite phrases to browse on Google always ended with the word 'free' because your girl couldn't afford to keep up with her habits. I built my personal collection of pirated books and ensured I had access on all my devices. It was a trend that started slowly but surely and gained momentum.

One day I woke up and like BF. Skinner's rat, I was thoroughly trained and conditioned. Masturbation had me in a headlock, and in exchange for total control, unlocked my chains of restraint and rewarded me with false freedom. I slowly plucked up the courage to explore new territories. I ditched the now tame Mills and Boon and Harlequin novels and delved into darker novels, all in the name of getting my next illicit fix.

I was a bona fide junkie, and it was only a matter of time before I needed a higher high. My choice of exotic romance cocktails no longer gave me the thrill or rush I needed. I knew I needed to explore deeper and darker sexual back alleys to feel the thrill and get a release from the urges that rode me. I toyed with the idea of watching porn for weeks but hesitated. That somewhat annoying killjoy, otherwise known as my conscience, cautioned me: *once you go there, it will be hard for you to come back.*

It is said idle hands are the devil's workshop, and an idle mind his playground. That proved to be true for me. One day, I was lazing about, not doing anything in particular, and I caved. I opened Google in incognito mode, so if anyone searched my computer history they wouldn't find anything. I swiftly typed into the search bar the phrase I'd had in my head for weeks and hit enter. I jumped down Alice's rabbit hole into a wonderland of porn, and my life transformed. My eyes and spirit were opened to a whole other realm of possibilities. I voraciously explored many of them.

Have you ever done something in the moment and then stood in the aftermath in horror and denial, shocked that you had done such a thing? The rollercoaster of emotions swamping your mind leaves you nauseous and repulsed by the mental regurgitation of your actions. That was me following each fix. I felt a huge chasm of emptiness in my chest and deep soul-wrenching guilt and shame. I'd take a mental whip to my back the morning after and chastise myself fiercely before begging God for forgiveness and promising never to do it again. I was ashamed to call myself a Christian, especially when I had to teach my Sunday school kids, lead praise and worship, or sing in the choir the morning after.

There was no panacea to alleviate the guilt and shame that plagued me endlessly. I felt like Cain, the son of Adam and Eve, with the mark and wondered constantly how no one else saw it. Surely the bright scarlet X emblazoned across my back was worthy of my own walk of shame and public chastisement, just as Cersei Lannister's was for her incestuous affairs. "Shame! Shame! Shame!"

I often contemplated opening up to someone, electing and de-electing possible confidantes. Then I would remember the poor church sister who had been openly ridiculed and judged by the ones who should have helped her get up. That thought quickly snuffed out that flickering notion. I couldn't chance it. I couldn't chance becoming a social pariah. I was convinced telling someone would mean the death of my social life, and I would certainly be ostracised from my pristine religious Christian community.

I was trapped between a rock and a hard place. It was lonely feeling alone and like no one would understand how I felt. Why would anyone else in the church be struggling or have faced something like this? Heck, they didn't even want to talk about sex! Surely, I was the only one who was addicted to masturbation. *How could you be so weak and foolish as to let something like that happen?*

But I couldn't possibly let anyone know how weak I was, could I? The image of perfection that was drilled into me early in my Christian walk and reinforced as I matured and observed how everything worked had to be upheld. Weakness would not get me into Heaven, so I decided to try to cheat the scales. I had to be a good Christian, but since I struggled in that one area, I had to make up for it by upping my Christian score in another area.

I viewed my Christian life as a math exam that had two parts, written and multiple choice. I had to surpass expectations on the written portion of the exam because I was failing the multiple choice miserably. So, I got busy being busy. I made up my score with good works. Whenever I was asked to take on additional church commitments, even if I had no availability, I would say yes but resent it. Isn't that ironic? I failed one part of my self-imposed test and resented having to do the work to pass the other part. The system I had created to get the score I needed to seem perfect and land a spot in Heaven was working against me.

One of the worst confessions you can make is, "I did it again." That vicious cycle of messing up, covering up, and trying to straighten up only to mess up again leaves you emotionally stranded and spiritually drained. It leaves a never-ending trail of mental castigation and shame, especially when you go before God and earnestly beg for forgiveness, only to find that you need forgiving *again* less than 24 hours later. *What is wrong with me? Why am I so weak? Why do I make the same mistake and fall into the same trap over and over again no matter how hard I try?*

Sin is missing the mark, and repetitive sin can make you so weary that you find yourself wondering if it's even worth trying to hit that mark at all. And that's the scary part because if you give up trying, what happens next? Isn't that what they call backsliding? And if you do backslide, how do you regain your spiritual footing?

This is the kind of dilemma you are forced to face when you're in a religious environment because religion leaves no margin for error. You're either right all the time (or pretend to be), or you become the poster child – a case in point – for "how the mighty have fallen." What then happens to the imperfect beings? And even if you could find a way back into the graces of the religious powers that be, you still have to deal with the Goliath of yourself.

Sinning big rarely starts out like banging firecrackers on New Year's night. It starts out small in the form of subtle temptation. And once you yield, it continues to get bigger like a rolling snowball gaining momentum until instead of you controlling it, it controls you, and bang! You're buried under an avalanche of regret and so deep in you can't find your way out.

You see, secret sins are not really secret. Even when no one else may know about them, you do. Your conscience serves as the prosecutor, detailing your wrongdoings from petty misdemeanours to the most sinful felonies. Your heart will take the witness stand and testify against you, and your emotions will be the jurors. *Your Honour, we find the defendant guilty on all counts.* The gavel of rightness strikes the hardened surface of your compounded failures, and shame and condemnation are swiftly executed. Your only hope is to be granted a pardon by the Judge.

My addiction led me to the brink of insanity and then pushed me over. This did not happen overnight, and I had to retrace my steps to find where things really started to go wrong. The defiant reading of romance novels was just a gateway, an opening that allowed stronger vices to clamp me in their grip. But there was something else that prompted that defiance, and I needed to find out what it was. I needed help – someone who could help me identify the source of this struggle and snatch me back to sanity, and the only person who could rescue me was the one with whom I felt the most disconnected. I was about to be granted an audience with the Judge, and I was terrified.

2

GAME OF PRETENSE

One balmy afternoon in the late 90s, a seven-year-old girl in a flowing summer dress dashed into the kitchen to ask her mommy an urgent question.

"Is he here yet?"

"No. Chanel, go take a seat before you ruin your dress."

"But you said he'd be here by 2:00! It's now 2:15."

"Go sit and wait. I'm sure he is on his way."

Obedient but sullen, she plods to the living room and plops down on the couch closest to the window that gives a view of the quiet road. Minutes later, she jumps at the sound of a passing car and spins to look out the window before slumping back into the couch. It was not him.

In the following fifteen minutes, she repeats the action again and again and again. Finally, she hears the sound of a car outside the house. She jumps up and runs to the window just in time to see the steel grey of her father's Toyota Camry.

"He's here! Mommy! He's here!"

She races to meet him before halting shyly to peer up at the tall, stout man before her. Her words get locked in her throat as her fingers twist nervously in her damp palm behind her back.

"Hello, Daddy." He's a stranger, but still her beloved daddy. That little girl was me.

Growing up, my single mother would state matter-of-factly to anyone who listened, "I know she loves her daddy more than me." And she was probably right. I loved and adored this man I barely knew. He was my idol. But there was a terrible secret I held dear. I feared him equally as much as I loved him because I didn't know him. We never laughed, played, or joked together. We never fought. We never created the space where I could be myself and he himself. We never talked. He never told me he loved me or made me feel safe and secure in his presence. The few times we spent together were always uneasy as I watched him with a mingled awe of his presence and fear of what I heard he was capable of.

He was never my "daddy." Before I met him, all I had to rely on was the blemished picture painted by the strokes of my mom's bitter and less than stellar comments. He was simply a man I rarely heard about and met four or five times before his untimely death that broke my eight-year-old heart.

After that, I carried a legacy he unintentionally left behind. I viewed all men with an air of suspicion. I was unsure of what to expect from them, so when in their presence, I demonstrated the nervousness of a flighty pigeon. Because of this, I struggled to connect on a personal level. It was a legacy that distorted my perception of God long before I had a relationship with Him. Though divine, I viewed Him through the badly skewed lens I used to measure men.

And then religion came along. Like my mother's bitter introduction of my earthly father, religion used its murky brushstrokes to present a portrait of God as the Dreadful Judge who monitored all my movements. "His eyes are in every place beholding the evil and the good." Coincidentally, this mantra from Proverbs 15:3 became one of my favourite scriptures in the Bible and served as a constant reminder that

"God sees all," so I should strive to maintain an image of perfection always.

My mind tended to focus on the judgmental and punishment-ready image of God that religion painstakingly engraved on my young impressionable Christian heart and mind. The assurances that He is a "good, good Father" meant little to me. I had no one who exemplified that image. I, however, knew exactly what someone who regularly judged and doled out consequences looked like. I saw it every day.

The passionate sermons of exuberant preachers and teachers burdened me with heavy cautions to respect (fear) Him because He has the means to deem me worthy and bless me with the desires of my heart. Or, at any given moment, He could judge me unworthy, bang His gavel and rain down curses on my unsuspecting head or land me in Hell.

The few times I opened my Bible, that was the image I focused on. I had read the story of God sending poisonous snakes to kill the disobedient Israelites in the wilderness. I decided to strive harder to be more obedient to the religious rules out of fear that God would do the same to me or worse. *I had to be perfect.*

I had read the story of Adam and Eve being cast out of the Garden of Eden and resolved in my heart that I would never give God an opportunity to cast me out from anywhere. *I would be in control.* I read the story of Noah and the ark, where only eight people did not drown. I thanked my lucky stars that God was no longer in the business of killing off the entire world using water. I only had to worry about going to Hell, a worry that rested heavily on my mind ever since I heard my first "Hell" sermon.

The preacher, dripping with sweat, clutched the microphone like a sword in the heat of battle and shouted.

"Hell! Hell! Whether you're ready or not, you're going to *Hell!*"

The thoughts of brimstone and fire, constant weeping, wailing, gnashing of teeth, and everlasting darkness, burning, and torment etched in my mind and gave me nightmares. I resolved to do my best not to go there because if I hated getting burned accidentally during my forays in the kitchen, I'd hate Hell even more. *I would do a lot more good works.*

Over time, striving to be perfect, in control and doing good works caused me to regard everything bad that happened to me as either the devil's work or I blamed myself because I had somehow displeased God and was receiving the punishment I justly deserved. "I was bad," "I'm unworthy," or "I'm not good enough" were my constant state of mind. Unsure of which reasons caused my misfortunes, I resolved in my heart to chase after a relationship with the Dreadful Judge the only way I knew how: make Papa happy by trying harder to please Him through good works.

That decision is a heavy burden to carry. It leaves you drained and unsure most of the time. *How did everyone else who testified about their relationship with God keep up?* It seemed they had a secret formula for a relationship with God that was only for a privileged few, and you aren't one of them. You can't help but think you must be doing something wrong because no matter how much good works you do, you always fall short. That knowledge makes you self-conscious and makes you feel unworthy.

The truth is we fall short because our knowledge of how to have a relationship with Christ falls short. My religious view of God as the Dreadful Judge, along with my skewed view of Him as a man to be viewed with suspicion, warped my motives for having a relationship with God. I thought I knew Him, but it couldn't have been further from the truth. I knew *of* Him. He wasn't Chanel's God; He was the God religion presented to me.

In sixth grade, I had a teacher who was very passionate about getting our class ready for the examination that would determine the high school we were admitted into. Well-meaning as she was, she wanted all of us to attend the best high schools. So, she devised a method to reinforce our memory of our 1-15 multiplication timetables ahead of our Mathematics exams. Every day after lunch, she lined us up outside the classroom door. We gained entry only after we successfully recited our 1-15 times tables. Wherever we failed or messed up, we were guaranteed to get a lash from her well-worn brown leather belt for each one we couldn't finish.

On the first day of this new rule, I learned all the way up to 13 x 10 = 130, but I kept messing up at 13 x 11. No matter how hard I practised, I always drew a blank at that point. That day, I earned three slaps from her brown leather belt. One for stopping at 13 and the other two because stopping at 13 meant I could not progress to 14 and 15. I didn't cry, but my red-streaked throbbing hand and terrified mind carried the bruises of the experience. I determined in my heart that I would never mess up again. I never got another lash.

Like that experience, the motives behind my relationship with God and wanting to do well were tainted by fear of the consequences. I did not want to get hit by God's big brown leather belt. So, I became a goody-two-shoes Christian, not because I loved my Father, but because I feared inciting His wrath and having to face the consequences. I believed if I messed up, the Dreadful Judge would punish me or kill me and damn my soul for eternity.

The people we least want to be around are those we fear will kill, hurt, or punish us. That's the same reaction we have to a relationship with God, the Judge. I was afraid and unsure about how to approach Him. The formalities and strain to try to be well-spoken, perfect, and religiously correct in His presence drained me like a well-squeezed orange. So, I did the next best thing – I avoided the experience as much as I could. I didn't see a relationship with Him as important, and, quite frankly, I did not want to do it, which only reinforced my position.

Have you ever done something everyone says you should do, but, in your heart of hearts, you truly don't want to do it or see the criticality of it? So you do it but half-heartedly or mentally cuss the whole time? That was how I treated my relationship with God. People told me a relationship with God was important, but I saw it as just another annoying chore to add to my growing list of religious duties. One more thing that, if I got it right, would perhaps please the Judge or increase my score in the good works column.

For something so purportedly important, it was quite interesting that everyone said I should do it, but nobody ever thought to tell me why. I truly didn't understand the need or importance of having a relationship with God. I did not see why I was encouraged to spend time with Him daily or to spend time in His Word. I was busy enough as it was and didn't have time for optional things like spending time with God. I did not understand why I was encouraged to entertain the things that fed my spirit and soul. I couldn't crack the code the Bible was written in. And after a long day, I did not want to consume anything that made my brain hurt. I preferred to relax with one of my favourite books or movies. So, I chose to rely heavily on Sunday church sermons and a word from my favourite YouTube Christian speakers rather than spend time with God.

I did not understand the need for a close relationship with God, so I treated Him as an optional and a major inconvenience. I left Him in the back of the closet of my life and only pulled Him out on Sundays or for special occasions and emergencies. He got attention when I remembered and had time for it, needed to put on a show, or had nothing else to do.

I secretly avoided praying like the plague because, to me, it was just sitting for too long and saying a mix of fancy words that came from my head and rarely my heart. I learned the ACTS – Adoration, Confession, Thanksgiving, and Supplication for others – method of praying and clung to it for dear life. In fact, if I did pray in private, it was normally because I needed something and could not see how to get it on my own. I treated God like a slot machine. If I put in any effort, I expected to get something in return. So, I bargained, "Lord, give me something, and I'll do something in return." That was how I gave up masturbating for my entire 18th year. I told God I'd stop masturbating and delete my romance novel collection if He gave me something I deeply desired. He held up His end of the bargain. I broke my promise after a year.

While my private relationship with God sucked, I mastered the art behind the saying, "What happens at home, stays at home." I had a PhD in pretending I had an intimate relationship with God. While praying in public left me sweaty and nervous to the core – especially if I didn't get a chance to rehearse my speech ahead of time – I knew how to pray up a storm, in and out of my heavenly language. Everyone believed the lie I sold to the point where I believed it too.

But the truth was, even if I wanted to connect with Him deeper, I never knew where to begin. I felt like there were secret Christian 101 classes that no one told me about, so I neglected to take them. These classes were totally different from the Beginner Christian classes that focused on teaching you the principles of the denomination. No one ever told me *how* to connect with this Heavenly Father with whom I "should have a relationship." I guess they either assumed I'd figure it out like they did, or they hadn't yet figured it out themselves and so couldn't share. So, my private Connection with God 101 class became trial and error.

God certainly did not speak to me in the way I heard other people say He spoke to them. If He spoke to me in the still, small voice He used with Elijah, I never heard Him. He certainly had never spoken to me in the thundering voice that caused the Israelites at Mount Sinai to shake with fear and astonishment and wisely keep their distance.

Since I did not hear God, there were times I would test to see if He heard me. I would beg for a direct word from Him, even if it came direct to me via one of the Sunday preachers. On those Sundays, my heart would race whenever the preacher started making his rounds through the congregation. I was equally anxious about the possibility of hearing a word from Him and getting rebuked for my sins. Either way, it would at least have been evidence that God saw and heard me. Much to my disappointment, I did not receive the confirmation I eagerly expected.

I tried speaking to Him but was never sure if He answered because I had no tangible proof except for the times when I played Gideon. I asked Him to tell me which way to go by either allowing something to happen or not allowing it to happen. "God, if the answer is 'YES,' let the coin flip to heads. If it's 'NO,' let the coin flip to tails." My favourite coin to flip was asking God to let it rain or not based on His approved outcome. None of these things ever brought me closer to connecting with God. Rather, they revealed another truth.

My lack of connection and relationship with God and skewed view of Him made me feel like I couldn't approach Him and expect a gracious response. I couldn't shake the image of the God that my previous experiences had moulded and cemented. If I came before Him to confess a sin like masturbation, a sin that not even the church spoke about beyond "don't have sex" and "sexual immorality is wrong," I was certain I was going to be judged harshly beyond the point I could bear. If His representatives on earth would tear me to shreds with their judgement, wasn't He bound to be much worse?

My perception of God was not like Chief Judge Frank Caprio, the rosy-cheeked eighty-year-old municipal judge in Rhode Island who went viral for issuing compassionate sentences such as community service or a second chance. There was no way that the God of judgement who killed all those Egyptians at the Red Sea because of Pharoah's hard-hearted defiance and the Israelites in the wilderness because of their disobedience would want anything to do with a pretend Christian like my sinful self.

I feared my Father so badly that messing up made me queasy with dread. In those moments, I only had one thought, "Oh crap, my Dad is going to kill me." In fact, I often resolved that no one, including God, would ever find out from me, a ridiculous resolve to have when God is said to be all-knowing and present everywhere.

Aside from the fear, another set of chains wrapped themselves around me tightly: gut-wrenching guilt and shame. Have you ever done something bad to someone you knew didn't deserve it or would be hurt if you confessed what you'd done? You cannot bear to see the hurt in their eyes when the words come out that you believe will alter their perception of you forever. And you dread what they'll say in response to your confession. The words get stuck in your throat, leaving you swallowing rapidly to clear the blockage. Your stomach cramps in knots of nerves as your brain races to find the right words and the courage to tell them and then say, "I'm sorry."

When you feel like you're the only one who fails to meet the mark of perfection, you become the black sheep in your own eyes. And so, you never find the courage to confess or approach the throne of the Judge to face the music you dread. Each time you sin, deep soul-wrenching guilt and shame envelop you, making it difficult to lift your eyes and say, "Lord, it's me. I messed up."

You begin to think *there is no way He'd want anything to do with someone like me who pretended to honour His name and ways but didn't and couldn't.* And so, many times, you give up. So, you don't even bother to pray. *What's the use?*

Kirk Franklin sang, "Why You love me so, Lord, I shall never know." But your resigned thought is, *He could never love someone like me.* So, you take the easy way out. Like Adam and Eve in the Garden of Eden, you clothe yourself with pretence and take the only option your pride and shame offer: hiding.

Pastor Charles Metcalf of Transformation Church once asked, "Is your view of God shaped by what we heard about Him instead of what we hear from Him?" The truth is many of us are taught a first impression of God that shapes all our interactions with Him. He's the God everyone has heard of, but few actually know.

In the movie *Up,* there is a scene where Carl is leaning on top of a mailbox watching his new bride, Ellie, carefully paint the finishing touches on the other side. Carl lifts his hand and looks in horror at the gigantic purple handprint he left behind. Ellie smiles and playfully adds her own handprint in red. Our perspective of God reminds me of that mailbox. We start out with a pristine canvas, and then the world and our experiences fill it with impressions of Him – some intentional, some not. For me, my perception of God began with my father, then my mother and the church. For you, it may have started with your family and friends.

Too often, those impressions inspire an unhealthy fear of God. We seek a relationship with Him not because we desire to but because we believe we should. We serve Him because we want something or feel compelled to do so to avoid the consequences outlined in the Bible for those who reject God. We play our part like puppets manipulated by the invisible strings of religion to perform daily. Things don't flow, nor do we desire or enjoy spending time in His presence. We force conversation with Him, and whenever we sin or something bad happens, our first thought is, "Oh crap! My Dad's gonna kill me!" instead of, "Oh crap! I need to call my Dad."

Whatever your view of God and your relationship with Him, one thing is certain: the view ripples and widens in an unexpected way. I was about to learn that the hard way because I was about to come face to face with someone harsher, more critical, and judgemental than the Judge Himself.

3

MY WIDE EMPTY SMILE

On August 11, 2014, the world let out a collective gasp as the news spread like wildfire through the media. Actor and comedian Robin Williams – a man known around the world for his lightning-fast wit, uproarious improvisations, and bringing life to characters such as Popeye, Mrs. Doubtfire, and the Genie from Aladdin – committed suicide.

To friends and strangers alike, he always seemed upbeat. But behind closed doors, Williams battled his demons in an effort to maintain his health, sobriety, and sanity. Though he struggled on a personal level, he sacrificed self-care in favour of getting the next laugh. He gave the impression he was in complete control, often launching into one of his crazy improv routines to steer the attention away from himself. No one dreamed he would end up like other artists who had succumbed to their inner turmoil.

Just before noon on August 11th, Robin's assistant found his cold, lifeless body slumped over with a belt strapped around his neck. The Marin County Sheriff's Office said it was "like he was sitting in a chair." The death was ruled asphyxia due to hanging. The sheriff's department also revealed that a pocketknife had been found near his body and that his left wrist had superficial slash marks, indicating that he may have tried to slit his wrists before he reportedly hanged himself.

While the stories may be different, there are many Robins in the world today hiding behind humour and a big white smile as they struggle to handle the pressures of life and the expectations of the world. Yes, even Christians. I know this because I was one.

Growing up, my most commented-on feature was, surprisingly, not my big forehead. It was my big smile. At church. At work. At school. On the street. It was the thing that drew others to me with exclamations of, "My! What a lovely smile!" But there was so much beneath the surface that my smile and fired-up happy-go-lucky demeanour hid. I looked happy and serene on the surface, but below the surface, I was paddling like hell and on the verge of drowning under the weight of everyone's expectations and the pressures of life.

At about six years old, I decided not to make myself a bother to anyone, especially my mother. She had enough going on as a single mom struggling to raise her four kids. We weren't dirt poor, but we were poor. We had clothes on our backs (mostly hand-me-downs) and a one-bedroom roof over our heads. We definitely couldn't afford any of the luxuries my peers had.

Mom made sure that we never went to bed hungry, but there were days when we had to force down food none of us enjoyed. To this day, certain foods make me feel nauseous on sight. One day, my mom made a new treat for us: a big pot of plantain porridge. I put a spoonful in my mouth and immediately felt the urge to spit it out. My younger sister and older brother beat me to the punch and voiced their distaste. I watched as the light in Mom's eyes became clouded with hurt, and her bright smile collapsed in disappointment. In that instant, I decided I would never be the one to eclipse her joy with pain. So, I swallowed quickly, burying my distaste for the meal and willing myself not to throw up.

I finally finished the entire bowl. As my belly gurgled and rumbled, I mustered my biggest, brightest smile and quickly crafted a bare-faced lie.

"It tastes good!"

Mission accomplished! The smile returned to Mom's face. But I questioned my strategy when she immediately asked if I'd like another bowl. My stomach recoiled as I politely declined.

"No, Mommy. My belly is full."

I had many "my belly is full" days after that, putting my needs on ice and enduring discomfort for the greater good. "Operation Ease the Burden and Cause My Mom As Little Worry As Possible" was in full effect.

I would go on to deny myself of many things throughout my childhood, even as my heart grieved aspects of my childhood that I missed out on. I missed chances to socialise and hang out with friends because I opted to stay home and tend my baby brother so we would not need a sitter. Over time, I began to feel like I didn't fit in with my peers. I did not bring up school trips because I knew we could not afford them, and I did not want to see the look of guilt on my mom's face when she told me no. I did not participate in after-school activities because I decided to help my mom after school with her second job. And when two ladies sponsored my lunch expenses throughout high school, I opted to save some of that money and use it to purchase my schoolbooks so my mom would have one less thing to worry about or feel guilty about not being able to provide.

One of the most heart-wrenching feelings in the world is pushing your struggles, needs, and desires to the bottom of the priority list as you work to make everyone else around you comfortable and have what they need. And doing it with a smile even as you silently wonder when it will be your turn. You lie and deny yourself for the "greater good." Each time I denied myself, my smile got wider and brighter, even as my cheeks ached from the effort. If anyone had taken the time to look closely, they would have noticed the tremble in my lower lip. They would have seen the sometimes glistening tears of unvoiced pain in my eyes when I said "yes," or "I'm good" when I really desperately wanted to say "no," or "I'm not good."

Putting yourself on hold to live up to others' expectations can make you feel like you are not good enough just as yourself. You walk around with boulders of expectations and responsibilities that have been dropped on your shoulders by everyone you encounter, including yourself. You feel you have no choice in the matter, so you say "yes" even when you'd rather say "no." Sometimes you grow to resent your gifts and hate the things you love because you're forced to do them out of obligation rather than enjoyment. And if you are not careful, you forget who you are and start to believe lies like "I'm not worth it," "I'm not important," or "I can wait." It's a wait that never ends and one that fills you with bitterness and eventually causes you to snap.

When you fear disappointing others, it's easy to bury your needs and try to be the person they expect you to be. You convince yourself that you are their last resort or that only you can provide what they need. That was what happened to me in my days as editor of my church's Annual Youth Newsletter.

I loved writing, so I was elated when I landed the gig. But after three years, I decided I had enough and was ready to resign. The Youth President convinced me to do one final issue because they needed me, and I reluctantly agreed. After weeks of back and forth with contributors, the layout was carefully designed, and each article edited. I thought the newsletter was ready, but it wasn't. I received a call asking me to make additional changes at a moment when I was totally swamped, and I snapped! To this day, the attitude I displayed makes me ashamed. They opted to make the changes themselves and taught me an important lesson: the world did not need my yeses to go on. It was prideful of me to believe otherwise. In fact, by saying yes when I should say no, I blocked someone else from stepping into the role they were meant to step in.

Saying 'yes' to meet others' expectations eventually caused another toxic tree to bear fruit: a need for external approval and validation. I wore "dependable" like a badge of honour everywhere I went. Everyone I helped, except my family, raved about my dependability and brilliance right before asking me to take on more responsibilities. I strove to be useful and use my skills to be who everyone needed me to be – the strong, responsible, perfect, and dependable one.

I strove to be the responsible high-achieving daughter who would grow up to help her mother and shift her family out of poverty. I tried to be the perfect child my mother could always count on and not worry about. I had needs, and I wanted more, but I shoved everything aside in the name of helping my mom. I strove to be the perfect student. I studied hard to the point where I cried the first time I got a C. I wanted to be the perfect employee – often taking on more than I could or should handle and, surprisingly, still going beyond expectations. I strove to be the perfect Christian, showing up and using my gifts for the Lord by actively engaging wherever the church needed me.

Over time, my self-worth became tied to getting everyone's approval and validation. If I completed a task and no praise was given or appreciation shown, I took it personally. I viewed it as a sign that I wasn't good enough or had messed up somehow and hadn't earned the approval I desperately craved to prove that I was "dependable, strong, perfect and responsible." My resolve was always to try harder the next time or make it right immediately.

Gradually, I began to resent being so dependable and perfect, especially as I became my worst critic. I was always anxious that something could go wrong. What if I don't live up to my responsibilities and everything that was expected of me. If something went wrong or I failed, I was my own personal judge, jury, and executioner. Under the eagle eyes of my self-criticism, my every action was scrutinised and cross-examined. Any mistakes, missing approval, or things found lacking were immediately pinpointed, and a harsh judgement and sentence passed.

I was spreadeagled on a cross of my own making and flayed alive by my own harsh criticisms. My already low self-esteem withered with each judgmental blow. *I'll make it right. I'll do it better the next time.* The only thing is perfection was a good goal on paper but nearly impossible to reach when I relied on my own strength. So, next time was never good enough. My self-worth died a horrible death, squashed flat under the unrelenting heel of people's expectations and ground into the dust by the judgement of my personal critic.

The lyrics of Luisa's song from the movie *Encanto* became my life's melody. "Under the surface, I feel berserk as a tightrope walker in a three-ring circus …. Under the surface, I'm pretty sure I'm worthless if I can't be of service." I felt pressured by the many expectations. I was ready to explode, but I couldn't because I had trained everyone to need me, and I had to show up so I did not let them down. Sometimes, when the pressure got too much, I had small eruptions. They emerged in the form of emotional moments where I spoke harshly or sharply to someone. I learned to shutter my tears because strong people don't have time to cry and shouldn't cry. That's plain weakness. Those chinks in my armour left me feeling guilty, especially when my inner critic got through with me. I had to quickly fix them.

I never even entertained the thought of asking for help

because I feared it would be viewed as weakness. I did not want people to think I could not be trusted with responsibility or prove to be a bother to anyone, so I figured things out myself. I feared showing the ugliness of who I was under my armour: scared, making it up as I went along, desperately paddling to stay afloat, taking scarce pleasure where I found it, and so, so alone. Surely, I would be judged or found lacking and unworthy if I let anyone get too close. Still, I longed for someone to see me, accept me, and want me for me, not the things I could or was expected to do, but I was terrified of letting anyone in.

I often wondered, if I could shake the crushing weight of expectations, would that free up some room for joy, relaxation, or simple pleasure? Would it free up space for me to discover who I was meant to be? I was terrified of finding out because I was sure the me I was meant to be wouldn't be enough. Everyone needed the version of me that showed up daily to serve their needs. Nobody wanted her. Nobody needed her except me.

I felt like I was the only one who wanted to see the real me, not the dressed-up, stiffly starched version of myself who endeavoured to do everything perfectly and with never-ending demonstrations of strength and self-reliance. That version of me came with a persisting worry that my fake identity could be unmasked at any moment.

Like Mulan, I stared in the mirror at my half-masked reflection and contemplated, *"Who is that girl I see staring back at me. Why is my reflection someone I don't know? ... When will my reflection show who I am inside?"* I was weary of the perfect, practised poses and actions that were expected of me. The high expectations I allowed myself to be tied to became stifling, paralysing and stunting. So much hid behind my wide white smile, and I longed to escape it all.

I wanted to know what I was capable of outside the role I played daily. But I did not want to try anything new for fear it wouldn't be perfect or that I'd be judged for daring to step outside the mould that everyone's expectations had created. I longed to discover and just be who I was called to be, perfectly imperfect, without anyone flipping out or wondering if something was wrong.

I yearned for the day when I could be truly in the moment and safely express myself without feeling I had to choose between being authentically me or abandoning my responsibilities and disappointing everyone around me. I yearned to feel safe in the knowledge that I would not be ostracised and that there was a safety net of people ready to catch me as I stopped being scared of myself and judging myself. I wanted the freedom to embrace the possibilities that come with being who I am naturally, and simply and proudly *be*. I needed the assurance that it was okay to ditch the fake version of myself that everyone expected so much of.

Those thoughts occasionally ran rampant in my mind until my reckoning came, and I was forced to face the harsh judgements of my inner critic. *You're too weak and selfish. Everyone has a part to play – something they have to sacrifice. Play your part and play it well.* My inner critic sapped me of all energy to do anything but fit in. I had chosen the "perfect and dependable" persona at six years old, and I felt I was stuck with it for life. Like Tris Prior in the movie *Divergent*, my idealised world had no room for variances. Otherwise, I'd be forced to face the wrath of society, especially the people around me who I'd disappoint.

I began to hate any attributes of myself that did not fit the picture-perfect image I had chosen. I could not look at myself in the mirror because I hated what I saw. Through the eyes of my inner critic, I saw every glaring imperfection and hair that was out of place, and she was not afraid to let me know it. *You're not good enough, and you will never be good enough! You need to try harder and do more.*

Trying harder puts me in a never-ending competition with myself and, unknowingly, others. I tried to one-up my dressing for church. I tried to outdo myself by acquiring professional certification after certification and degree after degree. I silently competed with others at work and hated whenever a new competitor entered the race and needed to be sized up. I constantly compared myself to my siblings and sought ways to compete to get my mother's attention. It was never enough. I was never the winner. In my mind, I was always second best. So, I avoided risks and stopped trying anything new. I took the road most trodden and did what everybody else did – nothing more, nothing less. It was a traditional path that was tried and tested, so there were no doubts about the outcome as long as I followed every step. And follow the steps I did. I refused to try anything if I wasn't certain of the outcome. I'd even go as far as to research every step to eliminate any possibility of surprises. If I was not absolutely certain of the end result, I refused to take a chance on something new.

There were situations where the decision to try or not was outside my control. I sometimes took business trips to manage projects that fell within the scope of my job portfolio. It was during one such project that my dreaded unveiling happened. The project went on for over a year and failed twice. That was just the evidence my critic needed. My critic branded me a worthless failure, someone who wasn't good at the profession that, up until that time, gave me so much joy and set my heart on fire. *I was a fraud, and finally, everyone could see it.* Now everyone could see the scarlet letter "F" on my breast.

My self-worth was battered and bruised bloody by the one person I should have been able to depend on to hold me up and cheer me on: *me*. After that fiasco, I shied away from running a project for months, and it probably would have run into years had I known how to say no to my boss. Each project that I took on made my heart jump at every mistake. I played it very, very,

very safe and double- and triple-checked everything with my boss and myself. I did not trust myself or my judgment. I refused to take a chance and run the risk of repeating the beating I'd sustained and reopening the wounds from my past failure. Furthermore, I did not need any more public proof that I was a walking fraud.

Occasionally, when things got too much, and the pressure threatened to bubble over the tight lid I kept, I'd find myself carelessly entertaining strange companions: suicidal thoughts. *What method would be the easiest and less painful way to die?* I did not want anything prolonged and painful. I wanted something that would be quick and to the point. They were short-lived companions, but every now and again, they would come around to tempt me. Only the fear of what others would say and the high cost of my burial stopped me from venturing down this road marketed as relief.

With that door closed, I did the next best thing. Like an ostrich, I buried my head in the sand. Busyness became my anaesthetic to numb everything that was outside my control. I kept myself so busy to the point where I no longer had time to wallow, muse about my desires, or mourn the part of me I couldn't show.

Living life to the tune of others sucks the life out of who God calls you to be. You live a life of anxiety swayed by the rhythms that others and your inner critic produce. You live life with your mask firmly in place, not a hair out of place, and every aspect of your makeup done to perfection. But there is something in the fine print that you failed to read and plan for. Wearing a mask of perfection is a full-time job that requires you to keep all others at bay. It becomes quite a dilemma, as sacrificing yourself on the altar of everyone's expectations means not letting anyone get close enough to smudge your flawless façade.

4

CLOSE, BUT NOT CLOSER

My boss and I had been sitting across from each other in a boardroom, comfortably exchanging opinions about the merits of a consulting approach we were considering for a client. She stopped suddenly, resting her clasped hands on the table in front of her and staring intently at my face before dropping a bombshell of a statement.

"Chanel, you know, you are excellent at what you do, but I feel like I know you, but I don't know you."

I shifted uncomfortably in my seat and trained my gaze on the whiteboard behind her. *Where had that come from? Had someone turned down the AC?* The light and vibrance from the previous discussion drained from my face leaving a forced, awkward smile in its place. I twiddled my thumbs under the table and went mute as I waited for her to continue.

"You remind me so much of my younger self that it's almost like looking in a mirror. And so it is no surprise that I am having the same conversation with you that my boss did with me at my going away party when I was your age."

She leaned in and looked at me intently.

"Chanel, you have done excellent work over the years, and I

recommend you highly. But I know nothing about you on a personal level. I don't know you. I don't know anything about you, and I would love to change that."

We were having such a great discussion before. Why was she bringing this up now? What did she want from me? How do I respond to her? Panicked questions raced through my mind at 200 miles per hour. I silently wondered what to say and, for the life of me, came up blank. Still refusing to make eye contact, I managed to squeeze out a few carefully measured words.

"Okay. I'll – *try.*"

My boss opened her mouth to continue and then paused mid-thought. She closed her mouth and gave me a measured gaze. Then, seeming to draw some conclusion, she redirected the conversation back to our previous discussion about the client.

I breathed a mental sigh of relief. The awkward moment lifted, but like the stark impression of a well-placed unexpected slap, the lesson remained, leaving its red palmprint across my unsuspecting heart.

My boss, Marcelle, was right. I had perfected the art of keeping everyone at bay. And I wasn't fooling anyone.

Have you ever looked around you and felt all alone in the world though you are surrounded by people who are meant to be your community? You're in the community but not of the community. You stand with your face pressed against the glass window of life and watch as others play and interact on the other side. But you cannot join in for fear that those interactions will reveal the duct-taped, hideously pieced-together version of you. You hide even more, scared to death that your mask will be accidentally ripped off and you'd be outed for being the fake you are, far from the perfect version you show daily.

It is the loneliest feeling in the world to be part of a community but still external to it. You look on in envy and near-desperate longing. Everyone is connected with each other with cords that seemingly cannot be broken, but all you have are flimsy threads. Everyone has friends they can have inside jokes and secrets with, but you feel like you have to keep everything under lock and key. You connect with others but far above the deep level that your heart and soul long for. Everything is kept on the surface.

That was another reality my cheery wide-white smile and happy-go-lucky personality hid. I deliberately avoided any connection that might create an unbreakable cord. Like a clam in the murky depths of the sea, I learned to take in what I needed and give what was necessary without letting my pearls loose.

I got so good at maintaining surface relationships that pride took root. I prided myself on my ability to keep my secrets and hide the true me within the impenetrable fortress of my heart. They had to be pried from my tight-fisted grasp, and I wouldn't release them without a bloody fight. Even the friends I deemed worthy were kept at bay. Everyone was an acquaintance, even if they wore the title of friend and family. Close, but no closer. Unlike the Arawaks of my native Caribbean home, I was always readily equipped to ward off invaders and protect my treasures from all threats. Anyone who ventured close was immediately labelled as a foe; white flag or family, I cared not. Nobody would get access to crack the façade I had worked myself to the bone to build. I fiercely protected my persona, yet the real me cried to be released, seen, and accepted.

I mastered the art of superficial conversation, sharing minuscule but deep enough inconsequential details that left them feeling like a mutual exchange had taken place. They knew me, but only the version of me I chose to feed them. They never saw beneath the layers of my makeup though I longed to let someone in and share my burdens. It was a conflicted reality because I felt like if they ever did manage to excavate the real me, I wouldn't be good enough. They would be shockingly repulsed and want nothing to do with the imperfect version of me. So, I could not let that happen. I could not bear the thought of being rejected, so I rejected them first. I clutched my pearls close to my chest and resolved to never let any explorer discover them.

No one would ever see my morning-after look. I would spend a few hours with them until the energy of keeping my mask in place got overwhelmingly tiring, or there was a high risk of the real me showing up. That's when I left. If I did happen to stay the night, I kept up appearances the entire time. I went to bed fully dressed, and, like Violet Jones in the movie *Nappily Ever After*, I would sneak out of bed in the wee hours of the morning to wash my face, touch up my makeup, and iron my kinky hair into knotless waves before making my way back to lie perfectly posed in bed. That way, my friends and family always woke to the perfectly made-up me. Not a hair out of place or blemish on my face. Nothing for anyone to discover and deem unworthy. Rejection and the already accepted disappointment of dashed expectations were just too much for my already cynical heart to bear.

Isolating yourself also means that you become self-sufficient. You become committed to flying solo and depending on no one but yourself, especially when you are bent on protecting your secrets. If no one can get it, it means nothing can get out. That includes your needs and emotions. Like the inhabitant of a well-guarded castle that's fortified for war, the rest of the world stays on the other side of the moat, and all your needs are catered to by yourself. That was a lesson I learned too early.

When I was six, my Sunday school teacher unwittingly

shaped a central view I developed around self-sufficiency and God's role in it. In imparting the lesson of believing that we are God's children and that He cares for us and will provide for our needs and desires, she ended the lesson with words that inspired me.

"God loves you and will give you the desires of your heart, even if you ask Him for just a sweet."

As any child with a sweet tooth would, I trusted her words and gave this God a try.

"Lord, I want the sweet my Sunday School teacher mentioned before church ends."

I never got that sweet, but I did get something else: the faith of a cynic. Tainted by disappointment, my seven-year-old mind reasoned that God was too busy managing the enormous world and did not see me or hear my prayer amongst the billions who needed Him. Later, and for the majority of my adult Christian life, whenever I urgently asked God for something such as books for school because my mom couldn't afford them, or upfront money for college, and He did not show up, my personal judge and jury concluded, *I was bad*, or *I'm unworthy*, or *I'm not good enough*. Unsure of which reasons caused my heart's desires and urgent pleas to go unseen and unheard, I resolved in my heart to try harder but not wait around for the Judge to come through.

I reasoned that, given His inconsistencies, I had to be my Plan A. I had to rely on myself because He could not be relied on to always show up when I needed Him. That belief also expanded to the people around me. If the God of the universe was inconsistent, surely man was bound to fail me. My biological father had already proven that. If I had no expectations of anyone, then no one could disappoint me. So, I took to asking little to nothing of anyone, even if I really needed it. After all, I could only depend on myself because when push came to shove, I wouldn't disappoint myself. The backlash of all this is that I was always tired.

It's exhausting to live a lonely, controlled life where you are the provider, sustainer, and recipient all in one. Your needs are often neglected or overlooked because everything is ruled by the strong hand of everyone else's expectations. It is draining to walk around with mental images of the multiple personas of the convoluted version of you while you strangle any part of you that doesn't fit that bill. It is gruelling to show up differently in different situations based on whoever holds the strings at a particular moment. You get tired of always being on guard and on duty, always holding your feelings at bay to ensure that there are no cracks in your public persona. It's an existence that sucks you dry.

The night I nearly lost my mind, one of the main thoughts that ran rampant was *I am tired and I don't want to live the splintered version of my life anymore.* As my entire body pressed against the bathroom wall of my second-floor apartment, my sane mind resolved that I would not end like this. *I refused to! Heck! I was stubborn for a reason.* There was too much to do; some things I already knew, others I needed to find out.

I inhaled deeply and forced myself to calm down even as my mind spiralled out of control. *What do I have control over?* I could not move my own limbs. I had no control over my own body. I could not speak. *What can I still do?* I could speak to myself. Though my physical voice was gone, I still had my spiritual and mental voice. If that's all I had, I was gonna use the heck out of it.

Since pleading with God had failed. I shifted to something more powerful: worship. My mind latched onto the only part I knew of Tasha Cobbs Leonard's song *Goodness of God*, the chorus. I found myself singing at the top of my lungs in my head repeatedly:

And all my life You have been faithful;
And all my life You have been so, so good.
With every breath that I am able,
Oh, I will sing of the goodness of God.

Image after image of God's goodness flashed through my mind. For the first time ever, I think I actually believed that He had been faithful. As I sang, something amazing happened: I regained control of my limbs. Though my movements were still robotic, I forced myself to walk rigidly back into my bedroom.

The song of God's grace and goodness fought through the thick mental fog and burst through my lips. Even though everything in me resisted, I was determined that whatever had me would not win. The resistance and its control were big, but my God was bigger. So I used the only thing He had restored full control of: my voice. I sang louder of His goodness as I fought the resistance in my limbs, opened my bedroom door, and headed down the hallway to my mom's room.

Those few steps down the hallway triggered events that were so well orchestrated that it could only be seen as God stepping in before anyone even knew I needed help. I was delivered, but that deliverance came at a cost. It graduated my mind from the things I once felt were important. It opened within me a stark realization of how quickly life could change. I couldn't die without fulfilling all I was meant to do. It raised a pressing need to uncover my purpose, the big thing I was meant to do in this world. I knew nowhere else to look to for answers but to the Judge who I held at bay all this time. *Maybe He could give me the answers I desperately sought.*

Little did I know, I was in for the surprise of the century. Before He could give me the answers I needed, He had to open me up to receive them. The Judge was about to take on another role that I had never seen Him in before, beyond the surface level of religion. The Doctor was about to perform surgery I had no idea I needed or craved.

PART II

I can be real with You
Say anything and not be afraid
You made me and You like what you made
You made me and You don't make mistakes
I can be real with You.

– Maverick City x Kirk Franklin

5

THE JOURNEY STARTS
WITH A SNEAKY GOD

The air hung arid and motionless as if waiting for the fated outcome of the chase. Sue-Ann Ellington's perfectly coiffed Dorothy Hamill haircut was in stark contrast to the rugged, rocky terrain. Her pink multi-coloured scrubs fluttered slightly as she scrambled up the hill behind two out of breath young women. One of them was me.

Sue-Ann was a stout woman, but that did not seem to slow down her pursuit in the least. The rugged rocky terrain was parched and covered with cracks that resembled dark veins. Her sinister smile played across her pursed lips, hinting of derangement and the black-hearted glee of a predator who couldn't wait to feast on the flesh of her prey. The knife she held glinted its murderous intent as she stroked the blade in anticipation of delivering a fatal stabbing blow.

Sobbing between raspy, breathless gasps, we hurried desperately up the untrodden path casting harried glances behind us as we tried to keep a step ahead of the crumbling earth along the precarious trail. By some miracle, we managed to lose our pursuer. The pathway ahead narrowed, leaving only the rocky mountain on one side and the certainty of plunging to their death over the rocky cliff on the other. Fearing that Sue-Ann might reappear at any moment, we decided to keep moving.

Up ahead, we noticed two male figures dressed in wide-brimmed hats and what seemed to be full cowboy outfits. Even in the dream it seemed an odd place for two men to be. But unfortunately, there was no way to avoid them on the narrow path, so we had no other option but to keep going. When we came to the spot where the men stood with their backs pressed against the rocky mountain, my eyes zeroed in on their hands. They were enormous! The skin was cracked and chalky white, as though using lotion was a daily feud that they lost. Their crusty palms bore the tell-tale ridges and calluses of decades of hard work. But it was their fingernails that really stood out. They were chipped and jagged and caked with layers of black dirt. Their hands were filthy! They repulsed me and screamed *danger*. They made my skin crawl, and I could feel anxiety creeping up my back with an icy chill. Still, I persisted.

"Sir, we need help! You have to help us! A woman is trying to kill us!"

I hunched over trying to catch my breath and calm my erratic, overworked heart. My companion launched into a long explanation which, for some reason, I relegated to the background. It may have had something to do with me fighting the haziness that threatened to overpower my vision. I refocused when my companion touched my hand.

"*Chanel!* They said they can help, but we have to follow them."

I nodded my assent, too out of breath to get the words out, and followed with the meekness of an obedient child. But I could not shake the feeling that these men were up to no good. *Defilement!* The ominous warning flashed incessantly in my head. *We had jumped from the frying pan into the fire.*

I shook off the warning and focused on winning the battle

raging in my body. Along with the haziness, a war now ensued with my bladder that was bent on embarrassing me. I felt relief when I looked up and saw a rickety house buried in the side of the hill. It was easily overlooked if you weren't guided to it. There was no way Sue-Ann would find us here! I felt a bit relieved when the door closed behind us, but my danger antenna was still up. First, I had more urgent matters.

"Can I use your bathroom?"

"Sure, it's in the corner there," one of the men pointed to the right.

"Thanks."

I hurried towards the small door that was almost hidden by the shadows. A fluorescent light fixture welcomed my entrance into the claustrophobic room. The overpowering stench of stale urine and faeces assaulted my senses, and I held my breath to still my stomach and its racing desire to retch. As I regained my composure, I looked curiously around the room. It played host to a sink on my left and a toilet on my right. Both were dirty and stained and covered with spider webs of cracks. The toilet was filled with a dark substance that I dared not hazard a guess about. There were rusty, sanguine stains around the drain and muddy drops in the sink. My eyes travelled slowly up the wall, and there above me was a muddy handprint, or was it mud?

I heard the baritone of masculine laughter coming from the room outside. I imagined the men were having a merry time carousing with my friend. I couldn't shake the feeling that things were about to get worse. The moment I was out, I was bound to be defiled. *I didn't want to be defiled.*

I decided to heed my instinct and looked hurriedly around the room for a way out, except there was none. The small window was barred by rusty grills that were too small for me to crawl through. Resigned to my fate, I decided I would have to brave my way out of the situation I had put myself and the other girl in. For some reason, I felt responsible for what happened to her. *Hmmmn. I don't even know her name.* The door creaked loudly announcing my entrance into the carousing happening behind it.

My heart hammered loudly, pounding with an erratic beat, and my eyes snapped open. As I tried to still my shaking body and warm my chilled skin, I glanced furtively around the bedroom, searching for evidence that the threat of defilement had not followed me home. My shoulders slump with relief as reality replaces my lucid dream.

As my heart calmed, I was plagued by the certainty that this was no average dream. *What the hell was I doing in rocky hills? They looked nothing like the mountains of Jamaica, my home. Who was the second woman? She felt familiar, but I didn't know her.* There was more to it than what met the eye. It had a spiritual interpretation that would change everything about life as I knew it.

I whispered urgently, *"Lord, what are you trying to tell me? Show me!* I cannot rest until I know why You sent me this dream."

I'd love to tell you that following my near-insanity incident, I settled down into a relationship with God, but that was far from the truth. My motivation to finally settle in with the Lord to get answers happened after COVID hit and forced me to slow down.

As news of the virus spread in other parts of the world, I continued on with life as normal as could be after nearly losing the thing I valued most. The terror of sleeping in the dark ruled my nights, but during the day, I was my usual self. Nothing altered the persona I had created and fought to maintain. Sometimes when I struggled to sleep, my fingers found their playmates in a game that proved to be a perfect sedative to lull me into a dreamless sleep.

Everything changed when the Jamaican government announced that COVID had invaded our shores. A British woman carrying the virus attended a funeral, and within an hour, hundreds of lives were irrevocably altered. The press conference aired in the middle of our workday. As I stood watching the televised broadcast, I could not control the roaring in my ear. The hub of conversation from my co-workers faded into the background as my mind focused on one thing: *our vulnerability*. There was no way I could control or protect myself or the people I cared about from a virus that no one could see that had already annihilated millions. The probability of me failing myself and others increased a thousandfold.

I made it through that day, but my fears refused to dissipate, and my anxiety was at an all-time high. The roaring in my ears grew louder as I became more exposed to the COVID-related conversations and opinions all around me. I could not escape.

Masturbation provided only temporary relief. Afterwards, I had to face the aftermath that had always been there but now refused to be ignored: an unlabelled emptiness in my chest. I satiated my physical hunger, but now the emotional one lay gaping. In my mind, I was about to fail everyone I loved, and I could see no way out of it. *How does one fight the invisible?*

I longed for something I knew was outside of what I could give myself, something I had no confidence that anyone could give. My professional growth and the praises of my peers left me empty. That emptiness kept me awake at night, a partying companion to the fear that enveloped me in its cold presence. I longed for someone to tell me that everything would be okay. I longed for someone to pull me close into a big soft bear hug that radiated safety and security. But there was no one to be found.

I finally caved beneath the pressure. As the country shut down, I shut down. I distanced myself from social media and all external forces for a week and did something I'd never done before. I decided to give God a chance, an experiment of sorts. After all, He had promised to be my peace. What I didn't factor in was that His version of peace was about to shake my world right down to its core.

My experiment started simply. I committed to spending one hour a day with God. Each night, I would get sit on the furry red carpet at my bedside and follow a six-step "hide in the arms of God" routine I developed:

1. **Block distractions**. I would turn off the WIFI connection to my phone and close my bedroom door so no one and no notifications disturbed me. Then I would get my journal and a pen.
2. **Worship**. I'd select a worship song from YouTube and sing along to it to welcome His presence and shift my mind towards spending time with Him.
3. **Pray**. I started by asking His forgiveness for the times I'd missed the mark of living according to His commands that day. Then I prayed for anyone who was on my heart. Then I would simply ask God to open my heart to hear from Him and show me anything that might be preventing me from hearing from Him. Sometimes this would lead me to speak to Him about whatever problem was uppermost in my mind.
4. **Read the Bible**. I would dive into the YouVersion app to read the verse of the day and then the passage of scripture that was part of my goal to read the Bible in a year.
5. **Listen**. I sat in silence and listened for the small, still voice of God to speak to me.

6. **Journal**. I would write whatever personal application,
   revelation, or prayer was laid on my heart from
   reading His Word and listening to Him speak.

At first, it felt awkward. It was hard to focus, and the silence was deafening, but I never walked away empty-handed. There was always a word of encouragement or revelation to be found in the time I spent with Him. I started to hear Him, but it wasn't easy to accept because I questioned myself and wondered if I was mistaking my thoughts for His voice. But I knew when He spoke. His voice had a different tone to it. It was truly a "My sheep know my voice" moment. Little by little, I started to realize that God was nothing like religion had taught me. He gave me a measure of peace and stillness that saturated my entire being.

A week passed, and my commitment to my daily meetings with God did not waver. The furry red mat at my bedside became my sacred place. I kept showing up at our spot nightly to commune with God. He was my safe place. Over time, though I had never experienced the full presence of that role in my life, I saw Him as such and called Him "Father."

There are scenes from *Redeeming Love*, a movie loosely based on the biblical story of the prophet, Hosea, and his wife, Gomer, that left me in tears, blubbering uncontrollably. In one part of the movie, Angel, the prostitute, sneaks away from her loving husband, Michael, and returns to the whorehouse he had lovingly paid her debt to be released from after she was almost beaten to death. He married her and brought her home. But a few months later, despite Michael's kindness and grace, Angel sneaks away from her husband and returns to the whorehouse.

Although he has every right to leave her in her mess, Michael does not leave her to experience the devastating consequences of the life she chose. Instead, he chases after her and fights through several men to take her back to safety: to home. But one day, Angel makes the choice to once again return to her whorish ways.

I wept as I watched because I could clearly see myself in those scenes. I was Angel, Jesus was Michael, and my whorehouse was everything I chose instead of God. It was masturbation. It was my job. It was my need for control. It was everyone else's expectations. It was every idol I had erected in His place. It was me! I, too, had gone through an unending cycle where I left home and Michael chased after me, fought for me, lovingly forgave me, and carried me home, only for me to leave again. I returned to what felt familiar to my heart, even though it was unsafe and desecrated His temple and our covenant. Time and time again, I returned to the jail cell of my lust even though it left me feeling empty inside, utterly desolate, bankrupted me spiritually, made a mockery of His love and grace, and broke my Husband's heart.

As the movie unfolded before my eyes, so did my life. For the first time, I realized the awful job I had done at being a Christian. It broke my heart to have broken God's heart so many times. From that moment on, my desire shifted from doing good and making it into heaven to pleasing my Father.

He finally had my heart. Now I was free to renew my mind and allow Him to transform my habits. But first, He taught me an important principle. *How I saw Him was how I saw myself and others.* For example, I had judged myself and others harshly because I only saw Him in His role as Judge. Now that I saw and accepted Him as Father, it was time to transform my mind and belief around how God saw me. I wasn't just another item on His to-do list. I am His daughter. I am loved and seen at all times, even when I see myself as bad.

The revelation landed when I read the story of Hagar in Genesis 16, verses 1 to 13.

1 Now Sarai, Abram's wife, had borne him no children. But she had an Egyptian slave named Hagar; 2 so she said to Abram, "The Lord has kept me from having children. Go, sleep with my slave; perhaps I can build a family through her." Abram agreed to what Sarai said.

3 So after Abram had been living in Canaan ten years, Sarai his wife took her Egyptian slave Hagar and gave her to her husband to be his wife. 4 He slept with Hagar, and she conceived. When she knew she was pregnant, she began to despise her mistress.

5 Then Sarai said to Abram, "You are responsible for the wrong I am suffering. I put my slave in your arms, and now that she knows she is pregnant, she despises me. May the Lord judge between you and me." 6 "Your slave is in your hands," Abram said. "Do with her whatever you think best." Then Sarai mistreated Hagar; so she fled from her.

7 The angel of the Lord found Hagar near a spring in the desert; it was the spring that is beside the road to Shur.

8 And he said, "Hagar, slave of Sarai, where have you come from, and where are you going?" "I'm running away from my mistress Sarai," she answered.

9 Then the angel of the Lord told her, "Go back to your mistress and submit to her."

10 The angel added, "I will increase your descendants so much that they will be too numerous to count."

11 The angel of the Lord also said to her: "You are now pregnant and you will give birth to a son. You shall name him Ishmael, for the Lord has heard of your misery.

12 He will be a wild donkey of a man; his hand will be against everyone and everyone's hand against him, and he will live in hostility toward all his brothers."

13 She gave this name to the Lord who spoke to her: "You are the God who sees me," for she said, "I have now seen the One who sees me."

Hagar had so many strikes against her. She was filled with pride, and her pride was the reason she was tossed out of her home. She wasn't a Jew, and by general standards, God shouldn't have even cared about her, especially since her son was not the promised son and was only there because of Abraham's disobedience. Furthermore, she was just a lowly servant who did not honour her mistress and whose circumstances were due to her own actions. Yet, despite all these strikes, *God saw her.* He still had plans for her and her offspring and loved her enough to send an angel after her to console her and set her back on the path meant for her.

As someone who messed up frequently and felt like my true heart went unseen by everyone, it was a joy and blessed assurance to know that God sees me. That night, I wept as I wrote in my journal:

"Even when I feel unheard and unseen, You are God, He who sees me."

Tears wet the page as I continued.

"You see my failures and my distress. You see me even in the negative situations I bring upon myself."

The Lord then asked me a question.

"Chanel, how do you see yourself?"

I figured if He sees me, He knows the truth anyway, so there was no need to pretend anymore. I wrote down the following in response:

1. I lie.
2. I am prideful.
3. I need to give more.
4. I don't steward my talents well.
5. I don't give You much time.
6. I struggle with unbelief.
7. I'm broken.

8. I don't trust easily.
9. I worry.

He then challenged me to focus my thoughts on how He sees me and who He has called me to be. So I flipped the script and wrote:

1. I speak and live in truth.
2. I am humble.
3. I am a giver.
4. I steward my talents well.
5. I am available and open to God.
6. I have and show faith.
7. I am healed spiritually, emotionally, physically, and mentally.
8. I trust others.
9. I trust God and live in peace and joy.

Reframing my thoughts was one thing. However, living out the thoughts I had written down was a whole other kettle of fish.

Have you ever heard the story of the man, his son, and the donkey? The man and his son were on their way to town to sell the donkey. They all walked side-by-side until they allowed the opinions of the people they met along the way to take precedence over their original intentions. As each person they met scolded them about how they did things, they went from walking side-by-side to the father riding the donkey to the son riding the donkey, then to both men riding the donkey. Before they knew it, the story ended with the man and his son carrying the donkey on their shoulders into town. When the townspeople saw this, they all laughed, much to the embarrassment of the man and his son.

That story shares the funny truth about living our lives to the tune of others' opinions. We believe that they and their expectations hold us captive and that we must live our lives dancing to their tunes because that is what's right. However, we are the ones who hold ourselves captive. When things are asked of us – whether by others or the circumstances of life – we have the right to say "no" when those things are not in alignment with who we have been called to be.

But first, we must understand who we are called to be and why we feel that need to live our lives being who others expect us to be rather than who we truly are. We can learn who we are called to be when our perspective of God shifts and we start to move in alignment with Him. When that shift occurs, He leads us on a journey to renew our minds and uproot our conformance to the world. This allows Him to transform us into who we are called to be according to His good, acceptable, and perfect will (Romans 12:2).

This shift does not happen overnight. Sometimes we need to

unroot and unravel harmful and limiting beliefs and behavioural patterns that we have held on to for dear life for years. Some of these are even generational!

Business Alignment Therapist and Biblical Mindset Coach Susan Fleming posits that neuroscience proves that approximately 90% of your life is run by your subconscious mind. This happens when your conscious mind experiences repeated patterns that your brain perceives as threats and designs beliefs and habitual behaviours to protect you from harm. Those repeated patterns are then uploaded to your subconscious where they run your life on autopilot, protecting you from anything it deems harmful and influencing all your decisions and behaviours.

Imagine all the hurt and trauma you experienced as a child still showing up in your life as an adult. Your life revolves around protecting yourself and ensuring you're never hurt again. That dad who left and broke your heart. That child who teased you because you were a nerd. The siblings who mocked you because you didn't quite fit in with the rest of the family – you were the odd one out. That family member or well-meaning family friend who continuously asked, "Why you can't be more like your older sibling?"

That was some of the repeat hurt and trauma uploaded from my subconscious alongside the beliefs and default reactions I used to protect myself. Once there, my subconscious ran my life on autopilot. I spent my life as a highly functioning dysfunctional adult who navigated the ins and outs of life through the lens of beliefs that were automatically triggered by my subconscious need to protect myself. That's why I built a barricade around my heart where people had to prove they loved me and were worthy to enter. It was to protect me! That's why I played small and hid just how talented I am. It was to protect me. That's also why I spent so much time racking up certifications and degrees. It's to protect me and prove my worthiness.

Many of your actions, thoughts and beliefs stem from your subconsciousness' agenda to protect you. It will remain that way unless God transforms you or brings those harmful beliefs to your awareness and takes you on a journey to exchange them for the truth He intended for you all along. That's all part of the shift to having a renewed mind that no longer conforms to the beliefs and patterns of the world. And because God is not the author of confusion, that shifting is a process that begins with something that agitates your subconscious beliefs and behaviours. That agitation becomes the catalyst for asking 'Why?' and the transformational journey begins.

Let's talk about the key parts of that journey.

THE AGITATOR

God is a gentleman. He will speak to you and stand at the door of your heart and knock, but He definitely won't break it down or force you to listen. Instead, He will send situations to agitate you or allow the consequences of your disobedience to agitate the things in you that are holding you back from being who He has called you to be.

The agitator is a one-off moment or situation or a recurring problem or situation that triggers you immensely and shows you the limits of your power and authority. You realize that the problem or situation is bigger than you and that it is humanly impossible to fix. Sometimes it makes you realize that you want something, but you can't get to it on your own. For example, COVID made me realize that my good job and abilities could not keep me safe or fix the dissatisfaction I felt with my life. Sometimes the agitator is the thing that you've tried fixing on your own without much success, often with methods that are out of alignment with who God has called you to be. For example, you fear being let down by people, so you develop a habit of shutting down or kicking people out of your life whenever they do something you don't like. You reason, *they were going to let me down anyway, so it's better to get rid of them now.*

The agitator is often the starting point to deliverance because it's the red light that brings you to a halt and makes you realize that you need help. It makes you realize that the problem or situation is bigger than you and that it's time to turn to God. For me, it propelled me towards my Helper (God). Once I went to God, there was a series of steps that He took me through. This didn't always happen instantly. Sometimes it was over a duration of time. Sometimes it took a number of cycles because I wasn't ready or the situation was complex with many underlying layers.

THE BEHAVIOURAL RESPONSE

The agitator always bears fruit. When you're walking out of alignment with who God has called you to be, you'll often have an illegitimate response to the agitator. Sometimes you'll be aware of it, other times you won't be, but there is always a response. This behaviour is one that we learn from others around us or create ourselves. But one thing is certain, it is generally perceived as a valid and necessary reaction. For example, you may feel resentful that you are stuck doing an activity you don't want to do because you said "yes" when in your hearts of hearts, you know you should say "no." Your behavioural response is being unable to say no and then resenting it. Over time that behaviour becomes your default behaviour. Before God can take you to the next stage, He will point out that behavioural response.

Sometimes, you'll discover the agitator and your default behavioural response in one go. Other times, there is a gap between when you find the problem and when you identify your default behavioural response.

THE VALID NEED

The agitator evokes a behavioural response because there is a valid need that we desire to be met. This is a need we may or may not be aware of or be able to articulate well. However, we still try to fulfil it. That means there is a specific need that triggers a behavioural response over and over again.

It is said that insanity is doing the same thing over and over and expecting different results. So, if we never understand the valid need that is not being met or become aware of the illegitimate behavioural response we displayed, we will end up in a cycle that always yields the same results. This is why the agitator is so important.

THE TRAUMA EVENT

A valid need does not necessarily mean it's a healthy God-given need. Some needs are created by the circumstances of life. Though valid, they can be rooted in a faulty belief that was birthed by a traumatic event. The trauma event is the moment that caused you to replace your belief in a truth God gave you with a lie.

THE LIE I BELIEVED

There is a lie you believe is true. It sits at the root of your illegitimate behavioural response that tries to fill your valid need.

Here is how my friend, Lisa Vanderveen, Emotional and Spiritual Health Coach describes that lie: "Oftentimes during trauma, both God and the devil offer to guide you through the effects of the trauma. If you accept the devil's way, you accept a lie over God's truth and give your consent for him to trigger your trauma at will. Other times, you get to choose between accepting God's truth and guidance or protecting yourself by making a vow. If you choose the vow, you believe the lie that only you can protect you. It sounds good on the surface but is detrimental to you. For example, a child may vow to never let her kids feel the abandonment she felt because her parents were never there when she needed them. But the truth is, you take control and become self-sufficient, never allowing God to work through you."

An even scarier thing is that these lies then become beliefs that feed your needs and behavioural responses. Those are the reactions that our subconscious triggers 90% of the time.

GOD'S TRUTH

If you believed a lie, there must be a God-given truth that you were meant to believe. What reassurances has God given you? What does the Bible have to say about the matter? This is the word and promise you'll need to hold close as you follow God's instructions and go on a journey to be fully renewed in your mind and life.

WHAT DID GOD TELL ME TO DO?

God doesn't start you on a path without giving you one or more instructions. For example, He told Abraham to leave Ur. He told Moses to return to Egypt. What steps must you take in obedience to overcome strongholds and be fully renewed in your mind and life? Don't make the mistake of believing that you'll overcome the problem or situation in one go or that God will show you all the steps to take in one go. Your journey will *always* be a faith move where each obedient step reveals the next step to take. Move in obedience and watch as God snatches you from the jaws of the strongholds that had you bound so you can walk freely in the truth He meant for you and embrace your purpose.

THE PROCESS TO FREEDOM

When you obey God's instructions, a journey to deliverance or freedom typically ensues. The process to freedom may look different for each person. It all comes down to how willing you are to do what God instructed you to do and the journey it takes you on. Just know one thing: as long as you remain true to the process, you will reach a destination beyond your wildest imagination.

It's also important to realize that the process to freedom is not always a straight path. Sometimes you'll mess up and disobey or stall. But don't beat yourself up. Remember, your Father is full of grace and is waiting to guide you back on track. He'll even use your detour for your good.

Making the decision to relinquish your need for control and choosing to follow God's instructions and trust that He has you covered changes everything. God sets you up for a life that is exceedingly abundantly above anything that you could ever hope or begin to imagine. All He needs is your willingness to follow His leading, and He will take you on the path that He always had planned for you.

Like the wise builder who builds his house on the rocks, God painstakingly and lovingly lays the foundation for a journey that you could never imagine. And because the right foundation is laid by the Master Creator Himself, it sets you on an epic journey that goes beyond your wildest dreams. It brings healing and restoration as He shows you the areas of your life where you unintentionally became a co-conspirator with the devil's plan to steal and destroy your voice. It aligns you to be who He always intended you to be – a child made in His image, a child in whom He is well pleased, a child whose voice is full of purpose and blessed and empowered to impact and influence others.

6

IN SEARCH OF STRONGHOLDS

Your deep need to meet others' expectations wears a mask. It's not what it appears to be on the surface. It often hides some underlying fear that sunk its claws deeply into your psyche and has been your puppeteer for longer than you can remember. You think you are the master who is in control, but you are no more than a puppet whose actions and thoughts are controlled by an invisible master you had no idea existed.

My master was my fear of rejection and abandonment. This fear was much more insidious than it seemed. So God took me on a wide and deep journey to unhook all the little claws and cut my puppet strings.

Jamaicans have a saying: "While man is planning, God is busy wiping out." It's basically a caution for us to not plan without aligning with God because God's plan for our lives is different. And though man can plan, it does not mean God will authorise the plan. As a bonafide planner, this is a caution I never paid much attention to. Instead, I made my plans and then bargained with God to see if they could be pushed through. So, it was no surprise that in December 2019, I sat down to think about my 2020 goals and excluded God from the process.

As I reviewed the list I made, my sense of satisfaction was interrupted by a voice out of nowhere: *what about marriage?* I hadn't given much thought to marriage, so I brushed the voice aside like an annoying fly and continued perfecting my list. I went on to have two more incidents where the topic of marriage fell unceremoniously into my lap. After the third occasion, I semi-obeyed the voice and added one line to my game plan for 2020: *God will prepare me for marriage.* A far cry from *I will get married in 2020.*

Has God ever told you something you thought you had months or even years before He brought it to pass? That was me! I heard what He said but didn't take Him too seriously. I mean, He took twenty-five years to give Abraham his promised son, Isaac. Why should it be any different with me and this promise that I wasn't even sure I desired? But I was in for a rude awakening.

I started spending more time with a friend around the same time God was hounding me. Before you could say *holy moly*, our friendship started shifting. I found myself praying about how deeply I should allow him to get in my life since he didn't live in Jamaica, plus I wasn't sure I wanted a relationship. I secretly hoped God would tell me it was a mistake to let this guy get closer to me, but instead, God told me to "slow down." He expounded:

- Although the guy and I were compatible, he was not ready for a relationship and needed space to learn, adjust and grow.
- The guy and I had much learning, adjusting and growing to do, so I needed to slow down, step back and seek God.
- Be honest with him about my fears.

- God would redirect my path if the guy and I didn't work.

I did not take it slow like God advised. Although the guy and I agreed to wait before starting a relationship, we went ahead and forged a deep emotional connection that neither of us was mature enough to handle. On the surface, our initial decision stood. However, under the surface, there were a lot of unvoiced expectations, fears, and assumptions that complicated everything. Little did I know that God would use him as a catalyst for re-evaluating the firmly held beliefs by which I had lived my life. We both had a lot of "learning, adjusting and growing" to do. The first agitation came a month later.

THE AGITATOR

I loved spending time with this guy. We could talk for hours without running out of things to talk about. Or we could sit in silence on the phone for hours. Each night a battle would rage between our desire to sleep and our reluctance to end our call. So it was no surprise when we fell asleep on the phone one Friday night.

THE BEHAVIOURAL RESPONSE

Under normal circumstances, it shouldn't have been a big deal. But this was a big deal to me, a woman who had spent years never letting anyone see me in a vulnerable state. To say I freaked out is the understatement of the year.

The poor guy woke with a beautiful "good morning" while my brain went haywire thinking about all the reasons this shouldn't have happened. *I was emotionally connected to him. One day he would abandon or reject me, and it would destroy me! I couldn't let that happen!* Still reeling as my mind went down a million avenues, I hurried him off the phone with a random excuse.

For the majority of the day, I pondered what action to take. Finally, I resolved to do what I had always done. I'd snatch the ground I had given him out from under him and detach first before he got the chance to hurt me.

I later sent him a text message. *It was a mistake and shouldn't have happened. I just can't do this.* He did not take my message well and did exactly as I had predicted. He rejected me, or at least that's how I interpreted his actions. He just shut down and disappeared. His rejection really hurt, even though I had anticipated it and knew I had triggered it. In hindsight, I realise I had really hurt him. I had no idea how to fix it, so I turned to God for answers.

THE VALID NEED

Falling asleep on the phone with the guy agitated my fear of rejection and abandonment. It evoked behavioural responses that were designed to prevent me from getting personal or vulnerable with anyone. This response was born out of my need to never be rejected or abandoned by the ones I love ever again.

THE TRAUMA EVENT

Although my father lived until I was eight, I lost him before I was born when he and my mom ended their relationship. Whenever he paid my sister and me one of his random visits, I pulled a lot of antics to get him to stay, but he never did. I loved and adored him, and I'm sure he loved me in his own way, but never enough to stay.

When he died it broke my heart. In retrospect, I realised that my heart got broken long before that. It got smashed. My father was the first guy who was meant to love me and show me what it meant to be loved wholesomely by the opposite sex. With that obvious failure, compounded by the pain of his death, I vowed that I would never again give anyone that power over me. That childhood vow was one of my earliest moves at being the devil's unintentional accomplice and protecting myself. My words had power, and they allowed him room to take up residence in my life and open the wound wider.

The devil took advantage of the fact that we moved around a lot when I was a child. At age seven, we packed up our house and moved to St. Catherine, Jamaica. That move, my first major one, resulted in me leaving behind my first and best friend, a girl I had affectionately nicknamed Kizzy Azzy Wizzy. Losing her, plus the reality of our constant moves, lessened my desire to make deep friendships because I knew, sooner or later, I would soon need to leave them behind.

Instead, I favoured the steady companionship of books over human relationships. I read everywhere (my poor eyesight is a testament to this) and took pride in my love for books. In primary and high schools, my favourite place was the library. I spent so much time there that the librarians knew me by name. However, the truth is I used my love for books to escape investing deeply in my relationships.

THE LIE I BELIEVED

I believed no one loved me enough to stay. Because of this, I came up with my own distorted non-negotiables:

- I must guard my heart and space closely and never let anyone beyond the barriers I had erected. But, if they did somehow find their way into my heart, I would hold onto them for dear life, doing anything possible to keep them close.

- I must keep everyone at bay because if they got too close, they would eventually leave, like my dad, or I would have to leave them behind, like my childhood best friend. Because of this, I mastered my ability to get people to feel like they knew me when few did. Additionally, when it came to dating, there were two simple rules that I would follow religiously: Rule #1 – "Leave them before they leave you." And Rule #2 – "Never let them get too close."

GOD'S TRUTH

We don't have to fear abandonment or rejection because God is our Heavenly Father, and He will never leave or forsake us. The Lord spoke directly to me on this one.

"Your father may have failed and abandoned you, but I, Your Heavenly Father, never will. It's time to leave your abandonment issues behind and become a full reflection of your relationship with Me."

"Father to the fatherless, defender of widows—this is God, whose dwelling is holy." - Psalm 68:5

"Even if my father and mother abandon me, the Lord will hold me close." - Psalm 27:10

"Our purpose is to please God, not people. He alone examines the motives of our hearts." - 1 Thessalonians 2:4

WHAT DID GOD TELL ME TO DO?

After I ignored God's advice to "Slow down," God's next instruction was "stay the course." No matter how I lamented and begged for an out, God stood firm on His instruction. I couldn't understand it at the time, especially when everything in me wanted to run. Each time I went to God, that was the instruction I got. My friends thought I was off my rocker and told me to leave this guy because I deserved better than a guy who did not seem to know what he wanted from me and got distant or left whenever things got rocky.

THE PROCESS TO FREEDOM

My friends were right. I did deserve better, but not only in the way they thought. There were many layers attached to my fear of rejection and abandonment that had to be peeled away. It couldn't all be done in one go. There were layers that I wasn't even aware of. My fear of rejection and abandonment birthed two unhealthy extremes, and I had only been aware of one of them. First, I refused to allow anyone to get close, running away or detaching myself whenever I was faced with anyone or anything that required my vulnerability. Secondly, I couldn't bear to lose anyone that I let in. If you had my heart, there was a high chance you also had my voice. I would disregard my boundaries, bend over backwards, and go out of my way to please you. I thought maybe if you got everything you wanted and no friction from me, you wouldn't reject or abandon me.

After I disobeyed God's instructions to "slow down," He wouldn't allow me to exit the situation by defaulting to running away. Instead, He used the agitation to heal me by facing the root of my agitation head-on, standing up to the two extremes and embracing a healthier path for my future. If I failed any of those areas, I would continue the cycle of people-pleasing out of the fear that I had held on to tightly since I was seven years old. I needed to understand the intricacies of what motivated me and deal with it maturely instead of nursing the fear or pride that typically drove me. I had to own my voice and stand up for me.

It took more than two years of missteps, emotional outbursts, pain, and rebellions to finally understand why God told me to stay the course. I had ignored God's instructions, but that was not all. I had also ignored my boundaries. I allowed my fear of being rejected or abandoned by this guy to push me straight into pleasing and meeting his expectations. I could not bear to lose him, so I accepted him on his often-inconsistent terms and ignored my needs. It was not that I was blindsided. This guy told me in no uncertain terms who he was and where I stood in his life. He made it clear that he would not get closer to me or give me a label beyond friend until he was certain about me. And though his actions often said something else, and I would go along with it, he always reverted to what he told me beginning. The heartfelt moments we had didn't matter. When they were over and things got rocky, he always reverted to the stance he took initially. *He is not fond of attachments. If bridges are burnt, he moves on.*

I spent many hours vacillating between pushing the guy away and then going back to apologise while sacrificing my needs at the altar of my forsaken boundaries. At times, a part of me resented him for it, especially when it felt like he did not automatically consider my wants or that I waived my wants for his without him even noticing. I even shied away from the "serious conversations" because I felt that he would leave the moment I called him out.

None of my sacrifices and concessions helped. He would go on to "reject and abandon" me many times. Some instances were real; many others were exaggerated and enlivened by my own fears, much to his confusion.

It took a lot of slow and sometimes painful stumbling to see what God was showing me. *You cannot operate fully in the purpose God called you to fulfil if you are overly concerned about being rejected. You'll drop your boundaries left, right, and centre in an effort to please people.* The lesson landed one day when God placed me in a sticky business situation that showed me that those patterns were not isolated to one area of my life. My fear of rejection and abandonment and people-pleasing tendencies seeped into other areas of my life as well.

A friend hired me to fulfil a capacity in her business that went beyond my services. Her business financial situation was tight, so we agreed to a contract that delayed major payments until the second quarter of our engagement. Everything went okay until she landed in unforeseen financial difficulties and was unable to meet her payment obligations for the third month.

A few days after the deadline, the friend told me that she would not be able to pay until closer to the end of the month. Given that a clause in our contract covered such a situation, I did not make a fuss about it. As that deadline got closer, the Lord woke me up early one morning and instructed me to have a conversation with her. He told me to activate the clause in our contract that stipulated I would pause all services if payment was outstanding following the end of that month. I resisted the move and went before the Lord many times. Why? Because she was my friend. It would be an uncomfortable conversation, and, most of all, I was afraid she would reject me. But the Lord was adamant.

Finally, the day arrived, and I had the conversation with her. Much to my amazement, she accepted the terms and thanked me for my forthrightness and for being an example to her. It seemed God had also been working on her, but it didn't end there. Upholding one's boundaries goes beyond saying you'll do something. You have to actually do it.

It so happened that on the day I was meant to pause my services, my friend and I were scheduled to have our weekly business meeting. She reached out to ask if we could shift the meeting down, and I responded with a reminder that my services would be paused due to non-payment. She didn't say a word. A few days later, I received two emails. One was a payment notification saying she had settled her balance. The other was a personal email from her thanking me for holding her accountable, being an example for her, and expressing a desire to rehire me in a capacity that fell in line with my services but within her budget.

When you stop letting the fear of rejection, abandonment, and people-pleasing hold your voice hostage, God will use you to free others. Lesson learned, but class wasn't over. I needed to prove that I had learned the principle: *I am loved, and I do not need to waive my boundaries to bribe anyone to stay. I can confidently and safely speak my truth without fear of losing the ones I love.*

This is where my process continues daily. It's not the easiest journey, but I'm growing. Sometimes I'd love God to snap His fingers and declare, "It is finished!" making me instantly free of this desire to please others, but that's not how it works. There is a habit that I need to foster, and God's chosen way for me to cement it is by practising it and triumphantly sticking to my boundaries even when I'm unsure how people will react or how things will turn out. Like my mentor who stood up in a boardroom and spoke her contrary beliefs even as her voice shook, I have to own my voice and stand up for me even when my voice shakes and my insides quiver at the unknown outcome.

You have a similar call. You have to stand up for you and do it continuously so you can flex your boundary muscles and kick people-pleasing and your fears of rejection and abandonment to the curb. Everything will not be perfect or done and dusted in one go. Sometimes you'll even fail – believe me, I have – but you cannot let it deter you. Quiet that harsh critic in your head and give yourself the amazing gift that your Heavenly Father gives you daily: grace. Brush yourself off and go again. Stand tall and beautiful. Own the beautiful voice that God has gifted you.

People-pleasing is looking for affirmation from the creation instead of the Creator. A focus on pleasing others often means displeasing God. You make people and their expectations your priority as you do everything in your power to avoid the pain of rejection or being abandoned. Eventually, people-pleasing leads to behaviours and patterns that ease God off the throne of your heart. For example, early in my interactions with the guy, in my journal I wrote, "Whenever we fight, I struggle to focus during my prayer hour." Imagine that! A human being took priority in my heart to the point where he interrupted my time with God. **Anything that has a higher priority than God is an idol.**

Here's another kicker that starts a trend into something you could never imagine! When you live up to others' expectations of you, it robs you and others. It prevents you from showing up fully as yourself. It robs you of the purpose and impact you are called to have. And it robs people of the chance to experience you fully and be healed, empowered, and delivered when they step into your sphere of influence.

Another trend emerges when you feel like you have to hide your true self. It isolates you from God and others. As you deny your identity to fit in and meet the expectations of others, it chokes the life out of the person you've been called to be. You become a performer. It stifles your truth. It causes you to lie. It silences your voice. Eventually, it awakens a desperate need to find comfort elsewhere and keep the loneliness in your heart at bay. God had dealt with my people-pleasing ways, but surgery was still in progress. I was about to find out how I handled loneliness and my need for comfort at the bottom of a bottle that added even more misery to my spirit and soul.

REFLECTION

Let's get God back on the throne of your heart. What have you replaced Him with due to your fear of rejection or abandonment or need to please others?

____

____

____

____

____

____

____

____

____

____

____

____

____

____

____

____

____

____

____

7

SEPARATING PLAYMATES

When we hide or make our true voices smaller to appease others, it awakens a deep need for comfort and release. We often fill that need by choosing a common but illicit way and shrouding our journey in the darkness of secrecy because we feel we can't share or ask for help without facing judgement. We create a web of secrets.

And do you know what sin loves? The darkness that secrecy offers. Sin thrives in darkness. It begins small but compounds like a bad debt with interest each time we appease its craving and tell ourselves, "This is the last time." Soon we are left feeling isolated as we try to dig ourselves out of cyclical rabbit holes of sin without sending a mayday for help, only to find that we are in even deeper.

Sometimes these cycles didn't start with us. We were only unfortunate enough to inherit it from our ancestors, or to unwittingly fall in or be pushed over the edge. Though we scramble with scraped knees and palms and battle the unrelenting pain of nails ripped off trying to halt our fall, the progression down the deep dark hole continues. And sometimes, we give up and give in because what's the use of fighting? We are going down, and we can't stop it. Why bother? If we can't fight our descent into the cycle of sin, why not embrace it?

In the words of the song from the movie, The Greatest Showman on Earth, *"This is me!"* so deal with it. The bruises are painful, and we feel like failures and crap but what the heck? Pebbles and small rocks slap us across the face, and we feel sore, but things are outside our control, so trying to resist the fall into the cycle of sin no longer matters. But that's far from what God intended for us. He doesn't want us to settle or live life as the painfully uncomfortable version of ourselves who struggle in the dark or hurt in the open. He wants us to be the full version of whom we are called to be, who can show up fully and say, "This is me!" without the hurt or shame that fuels our defensive mechanisms.

Sometimes, the only way to experience freedom from the cyclical rabbit holes of sin is to shed light on the darkness filled with secrets. Stop being silent and admit the truth, first with yourself and God and then others. That's what James 5:16 talks about: *"Confess your sins to each other and pray for each other so that you may be healed. The earnest prayer of a righteous person has great power and produces wonderful results."* You can't fight what you don't have the courage to face or admit. Let me tell you when things shifted for me in my battle against masturbation. It was when I started shedding light and sharing the truth. It's when the intriguing revelations about who pushed me and why I struggled were unveiled.

THE AGITATOR

A week after I had the dream about the dirty hands and the certainty of being defiled, it still weighed heavily on my mind. I asked the Lord constantly for an explanation. Finally, one morning at about 4 a.m., He woke me up and spoke to me clearly about the dream. My mouth slackened as I listened. And then the weight of the interpretation hit me.

"Wait, God, let me grab a pen and my notebook. I need to write this down!"

He stopped speaking, and I leapt out of bed, grabbed my notebook and a pen from my work desk before returning to the bed, and sat with my pen poised to write.

"Alright," I declared, "I'm ready!"

He began to speak again.

"You are running away, fleeing from things meant to kill you. However, you have also chosen to walk along a path that invites and puts you in contact with spirits that are meant to defile you. You are a virgin physically, but spiritually and mentally, you have broken your vow to Me."

My pen flew across the pages nearly as quickly as my mind tried to process what I was hearing as He continued.

"In seeking pleasure through masturbation, you have thought of and explored topics that have left you impure. You've willingly invited spirits that mean to defile you and allowed spirits with dirty hands to touch you."

THE BEHAVIOURAL RESPONSE

This type of agitator was one where the Lord chose to give me a wake-up call that agitated me without triggering a behavioural response.

THE VALID NEED

As a little girl, I used to suck my fingers and read to comfort myself and get a sense of peace. There wasn't usually anyone to hug me or tell me, "It's gonna be okay." So, if I got hurt on any level, popping my fingers in my mouth stilled and calmed my soul. But when I turned twelve, I decided that I was too big to suck my fingers and stopped. I had just graduated to romance novels which widened the door for a new comforter and prince of peace to step in.

Masturbating was a way to release or still the hot lava of volcanic pressure that swirled in me. Whilst sometimes the pressure was due to arousal, the majority of the time, a deeper need lurked below the surface. It was my panacea when I had a hard day. It was my escape and reassurance when I felt stressed or lonely or burdened by the expectations of others, or frustrated by the mask I felt forced to wear. It was my comfort when I failed to handle the emotions that bubbled up in me like a boiling cauldron. Like a momma singing her fussy child a lullaby as they sway to and fro in a rocking chair, masturbation was my go-to when I needed to feel relaxed and comforted. I needed a comforter and peace, and it stood firmly in the gap for me for years.

THE TRAUMA EVENT

I was molested when I was six years old by someone my family trusted to care for me. Feeling thirsty from playing cricket with my brother and our friends, I ran inside my mother's friend's house. My mother's friend's boyfriend stood at the door to their bedroom and beckoned me into a dark place I had never been allowed to venture into before. My mind screamed alerts as he tried to pull down my shorts. My small hands pushed his away, but his larger ones stilled mine.

"It's going to be okay," he said in a hushed reassuring voice.

I believed him.

I instinctively knew what he was doing was wrong, but I wasn't mature enough to understand why. My mind stood detached as he petted my vagina with his tongue and then touched me while he touched himself. Before my six-year-old mind could even attempt to make sense of what was happening to me, he finished and roughly drew up my shorts.

"Do not tell anyone!" His voice was a whisper but harsh with the implied threat.

I nodded my assent before returning to play. I kept that promise until I was well into my twenties.

A few weeks later, I tried to do the same thing to a little boy, and he told his mom what I had done. It caused an uproar amongst the adults, but no one ever ventured to ask me where I had learned it. After the chaos died down, life returned to normal for everyone except me.

My silence came at a cost. I blocked out that period of my childhood totally. My mind put up a big "DO NOT DISTURB" sign and blocked out everyone, including me, with barbed wires. I had no recollection of the incident until God brought it back to my remembrance at twenty-eight.

When the memory surfaced and flooded over me, I grieved bitterly for my six-year-old self who had her innocence stolen. From my grief stemmed anger at God. *He should have protected me!* That night, as I lay on the red carpet at my bedside, I wept brokenly before the Lord as red-hot anger seared through me. A broken little girl muttered incoherently between broken sobs.

"How could You let this happen? I was just a little girl! I hate You!"

It is a question I never got an answer to. But as I lay there in a posture of brokenness with snotty nostrils and tears streaming unchecked down my face, the Lord showered me with a sense of warmth and peace and reaffirmed His love for me. *It happened, but I wasn't going to break because of it.*

He then opened my eyes to another truth. That act of molestation made me very susceptible to sexual perversions, which was further exacerbated by my love for romance novels. My curiosity sealed my downfall into an area where He had never meant for me to venture.

THE LIE I BELIEVED

I felt alone and unworthy of being protected by anyone. I couldn't trust anyone, especially men, with my vulnerability because the very people who were meant to protect me had hurt me. I also believed no one cared enough to see me and notice that things weren't okay. There were signs of my trauma, but everyone was too busy to see them. So, I had to nurse my own wound. I had to comfort myself because no one else could comfort me or show me the love I needed to be comforted. No one else was there to ease the burdens on my shoulders. So, I had to carry it alone.

A small part of me also believed that I was unworthy and defiled and that no good man would want me. It fed my lack of boundaries when it came to the few men I let into my heart. It also made me feel like I was alone, not just in an isolated moment but probably for the future to come.

When it came to masturbation, a part of me resigned itself to the belief that my body and urges would always dictate what I needed. I had no control. I would pray and repent one morning only for my fingers to find their playmate the same night when the weight felt heavy, or I would feel isolated and alone, and in need of comfort or relaxation. Nothing I did worked, and I felt weak and alone in a struggle that I couldn't share with anyone.

GOD'S TRUTH

In July 2020, I watched a sermon titled *The Compromise of Pornography* from Transformation Church's Relationship Goals Reloaded series. I felt seen and understood for the first time as I listened to Pastor Michael Todd share his journey of being freed from the chains of porn, perversion, and the lies of the enemy. During the sermon, he said something that turned my belief that my body ruled me on its head: *"If God can raise a dead body from the grave, He can control a living one."* I felt empowered by the realization that I was not meant to be a slave to my body.

That realization opened up my ear to hear from the Lord.

- He reminded me that all things are possible with Him. He gives me the power to do what pleases Him, and He doesn't want me shackled to masturbation.

"For God is working in you, giving you the desire and the power to do what pleases him." - Philippians 2:13

- I have a Father who loves me and wants me to take my burdens and anxieties to Him.

"Casting all your anxieties on Him, because He cares for you." - 1 Peter 5:7 ESV

- Finally, He reminded me that He had already given me a Comforter. The Holy Spirit is my Comforter! He gives me peace that surpasses all understanding and makes sure I am never alone.

"But when the Father sends the Advocate as my representative—that is, the Holy Spirit—He will teach you everything and will remind you of everything I have told you. I am leaving you with a gift—peace of mind and heart. And the peace I give is a gift the world cannot give. So don't be troubled or afraid." – St. John 14:26-27

WHAT DID GOD TELL ME TO DO?

The morning I received the interpretation for my "dirty hands" dream, the Lord told me, "I am renewing My vows with you, but you have to let Me lead." He then instructed me to take two steps.

1. Share my story with an acquaintance.
2. Ask a friend to anoint me and my home.

THE PROCESS TO FREEDOM

Both instructions left me hesitant, especially the one where I was required to share my struggle out loud. It required being vulnerable before another person and running the risk of being judged, which defied everything in my nature. Like Gideon, who had asked God for confirmation, I asked God to let my friend call me if I was truly meant to speak with her about my masturbation problem.

She called me that night, and with a deep breath and a terrified heart, I launched into my tale. She listened without interrupting and then shared that she had once experienced that similar struggle too. For the first time ever, I realized I was not alone in my struggle. Plus, I could overcome it! It was not undefeatable!

Following our conversation, I was truly heartened and committed to overcoming, but it was still a struggle I dealt with daily. My heart and spirit were willing, but my flesh was weak. I felt that sooner rather than later, my flesh would win.

Around that season, the Lord started pulling on my heart with an extra special request: *wake up at 5:00 o'clock in the morning and spend time with Me.* Needless to say, I ignored the request. It was crazy! God knew I was not a morning person. There was no way I was going to do that wake-up-early thing. But don't you just feel loved and humbled when the Lord chases after you even when you can't see His plan and continue to reject it based on what you consider to be your limitations?

A week later, two of my friends came to me with a plan.

They wanted us to get together at 5:00 a.m. and seek the face of God. Again, I rejected the request with the same excuse I had made before "I was not a morning person." The Lord, however, was not to be deterred. A few weeks later, a Facebook acquaintance reached out to me.

"It's been on my heart for you and me to do a forty-day journey where we meet for thirty minutes to pray and read the Bible together."

That's when it hit me that God was definitely up to something, and I finally yielded.

"Let's do it!"

I was in no way surprised when she suggested that we meet at 5:30 a.m. We started two days later.

Halfway through our time together, I recognized two curious shifts. First, I no longer battled an immense desire to masturbate, and the Holy Spirit had shifted into the role of Comforter in my life. In fact, when things happened, or I felt worried and stressed, my immediate response was to lean into Him, hand it to Him, or speak to Him first.

By day forty, my desire to masturbate as a means of being comforted was totally gone. That invalid response I used to appease my need for comfort was totally gone! This did not mean I lost my sexual urges, those were normal, but I now had control of my body. I didn't need to masturbate to bring my body back under subjection, nor did I feel an immense need to. My body or sexual needs didn't run me anymore. The Lord and I ran it. The false king of my comfort had been ousted. The rightful King had taken His place as my Comforter on the throne of my heart.

The Holy Spirit is meant to be our Comforter. Jesus is meant to be our Prince of Peace. When neither of these manifestations of God is given the place to play those roles in our lives, we find other ways to cope and lean into our own strength whenever things become too much.

Some people drink wine and liquor to release the pressure and find comfort and peace. Some people take drugs. Some retreat into themselves. Others eat excessively, while others keep busy. I chose to seek comfort and peace in masturbation just so I could still the voices in my head, relax enough to sleep, and make it into the next day with the expected smile on my face.

And that's another thing. Though we run from it, a stifled voice will still speak. Many times, the voice we run from is not external. It's the one that lives within and screams loudly to be heard. Sometimes that internal voice is the version of ourselves that we have hidden away from everyone, even ourselves. It pounds loudly on the closet doors of our minds begging to be let out. Sometimes it's the voice of our worst critic who screams at us daily in condemnation or incessant reproach. Sometimes it's the kind voice of our Father asking to be let in as He stands at the door of our hearts and knocks, hoping we'll let Him into our hearts and lives so that He can be our lasting Comforter and Peace. Those are the voices we try desperately and often unsuccessfully to silence.

I've never liked failing, but being unsuccessful at silencing the voice of God about my masturbation habits was definitely one time when my failure presented an even better option. The chance to have everlasting peace and comfort without dying. The chance to be released from constant guilt and shame. Putting the Holy Spirit on the throne as my Comforter also eased open the door for me to handle other areas that had burdened my soul for years. It was going to be a rocky ride, but it cemented sweet rewards in my life: peace and comfort, the two things I desperately craved.

REFLECTION

Let's get the Holy Spirit into the place of Peace and Comforter over all areas of your life. What is the thing or person that is your comfort?

____

____

____

____

____

____

____

____

____

____

____

____

____

____

____

____

____

____

____

____

8

SUBDUED EMOTIONS AND SURFACE RELATIONSHIPS

My friend and I sat discussing an intense topic when the conversation took a turn for the worse.

"You know I love you, right? We've been friends for more than ten years, but I don't think I've ever told you that."

The other friend looks on, clearly uncomfortable.

"You're quite mushy today," she replied, fiddling with her hands. Clearly, she was in unfamiliar territory.

I looked at her knowingly. My friend was in a place I had escaped from. She was still not totally comfortable with her emotions.

Every time a friend calls me sentimental, mushy, or emotional, I wear it like a badge of honour because I now walk daily in the miracle that God gave me. I could be safe and vulnerable not just with Him but also with the people around me. Before that, I was an emotional dwarf. I lacked emotional maturity. I was so emotionally stunted that I couldn't even recognize my own emotions if they slapped me in the face. The idea of even expressing those feelings to someone else used to be laughable. There was no way I could ever do it. God was about to show me why nothing is impossible with Him.

THE AGITATOR

Remember that guy I mentioned in Chapter 6? He turned out to be both a blessing and a source of irritation and headache. When it came to my emotions, he triggered me left, right, and centre. Our interactions increased my frustration because I struggled to articulate how I felt, and he tended to shut down. It often felt like we played a game of who would be the first to express our feelings about most things, especially the important things. It was a game that truly frustrated me. At the same time, it gave me insight into how others around me must have felt when I shut down instead of handling my emotions. It was a bitter pill to swallow, but I recognized my part in it and longed for a way to stop being timid and speak up. But it seemed like a daunting challenge that I was in no way up for.

THE BEHAVIOURAL RESPONSE

Because of this, when faced with emotionally charged situations, I either shut down fully and let the tide pass, or I'd hide behind my bright white smile and pretend that everything was okay. Even as I bled and mutinied inside, I'd stick a band-aid over the gaping emotional hole and carry on with life pretending it wasn't there.

I was a true advocate for "what doesn't kill you makes you stronger." As long as nobody knew how I felt, I could live to fight another day. I had to live up to the standards of my culture, where it was considered weak to express myself through emotions. In fact, I held on to my emotions for dear life because I felt that I didn't have any emotionally safe spaces. Even when I was with my friends, I held back the depths of my emotions because I feared I would be judged as weak or considered ridiculous for losing control.

THE VALID NEED

I longed for a safe space to release my emotions.

THE TRAUMA EVENT

When I learned that my father had died, it destroyed me. The last time I saw him, he had promised that he would only be gone a short while, and when he returned, he would bring gifts and spend more time with my sister and me. As an eight-year-old who adored the dad she only saw once or twice per year, if that much, it was a dream come true. Like a kid in a candy store, I eagerly anticipated his return.

That year, my mom, siblings, and I spent Christmas with my oldest sister at my dad's house. It was a pleasant enough evening. We even took an idyllic walk down to the beach as we laughed and chatted. But it was the calm before the storm, and an unseen wave was about to crash over me.

The sun set, and we slowly made our way back up the steep road where my dad's house stood. I excitedly talked about looking forward to my dad's return. It was then I noticed that the adults had stopped. My sister looked at me.

"What you mean when daddy return? Robe dead!"

Dumbstruck, I stared at her as my mind tried to compute what she had just said. I rejected it immediately and continued in silence. *She had to be joking. My father was not dead. He had promised!* But the truth eventually settled in. *My sister wasn't cruel enough to lie about something like this.*

As the tempest roared through my mind and heart, silent tears slid down my cheeks as I tried to stifle the howl that clawed to escape my blocked throat. *He was gone, and he was never coming back!* At that moment, my mother looked over at me.

"What are you crying for? It's nothing for you to cry about."

My world had collapsed, and at the moment I most needed comfort and a shoulder to release my emotions, I was denied one and made to feel like nothing I felt was worth crying over. *The dad I loved had died, for heaven's sake. All the dreams I had of us getting close had also died with him. What was I supposed to do?*

The howl expired, leaving a painful lump in my throat, and I sobered up. I would go on to cry about my father's death many times after that, but whenever the tears threatened to come in the presence of others, I stilled them or wept silently so no one noticed. Only in the privacy of my own company were they free to be released. And even then, not too often, not for long, and never aloud because I feared someone would hear and ridicule me.

THE LIE I BELIEVED

Big girls don't cry. Big girls don't share their feelings.

To emote was a sign of weakness.

No one cared if I cried or would hold a safe space for me if I cried.

People found it bothersome when I shared how I felt.

GOD'S TRUTH

God is not daunted by our emotions. On the contrary, he wants to be the safe space for our emotions, and He is fully capable of directing us on how to share them with others.

- Jesus expressed sorrow at the death of Lazarus.

"Then Jesus wept." – John 11:35

- God cares so much about us that He keeps track of all our tears.

"You keep track of all my sorrows. You have collected all my tears in your bottle. You have recorded each one in your book." – Psalms 56:8

- God doesn't just care about us when the going is good. He wants us to carry our worries to Him.

"Give all your worries and cares to God, for he cares about you." – 1 Peter 5:7

- He knew we would experience other emotions, so he guided us on how to manage them. For example, anger and worry.

"And 'don't sin by letting anger control you.' Don't let the sun go down while you are still angry." – Ephesians 4:26

"Don't worry about anything; instead, pray about everything. Tell God what you need, and thank him for all he has done." – Philippians 4:6

- The fruit of the Spirit – love – and many of its segments are emotions.

"But the Holy Spirit produces this kind of fruit in our lives: love, joy, peace, patience, kindness, goodness, faithfulness, gentleness, and self-control. There is no law against these things!" – Galatians 5:22-23

WHAT DID GOD TELL ME TO DO?

God cares about all the minute details of your life. Yes! Even the things that you believe He wouldn't care about. That's why it is impossible to have a deep relationship with God and maintain a fortressed heart at the same time. A fortressed heart shuts out everything, even the crystal-clear voice of God. You can challenge me if you want. You can test it if you dare, but I stand by my words. The minute you get into a relationship with Christ, He begins to open you up. You begin to open up and find yourself sharing things the way you would with a friend. You literally begin to cast your cares on Him. And if you are hesitant because you don't want to be a bother or it just hasn't crossed your mind to do so, you best believe that He will encourage you to share in the safe space of His arms.

My first deep encounter with God encouraging me to share happened one night when I came into my time with Him heavy and wearied down. The day had just been too much. I felt so pressured that I could not focus. Ignoring how I felt, I launched into our routine.

I can just imagine that He watched me for a few moments, wondering if I was really going to pretend like nothing was wrong. But I persisted. That's when He gently stopped me.

"I can feel the heaviness on your heart." He said. "I don't want relationship with you to be a mindless routine. Talk to Me. Share your heart."

THE PROCESS TO FREEDOM

God's soft and gentle encouragement was all I needed. A floodgate of emotions opened up, and I blubbered and gushed out everything on my mind, even things I didn't realize were there. When the emotional storm ended, I felt so free and light. That's when I realized the power to be found in sharing your heart and crying before the Lord. But God doesn't just want our hearts to only be opened to Him. He wants us to feel safe sharing vulnerably with ourselves and others. And the thing is, if we ask for His guidance, He will guide us concerning when and where it is safe to share.

Remember that saying about how we see Him is how we will see ourselves and, therefore, how we'll see others? Sharing your heart and feelings uses a similar principle. If your heart is closed off to God, it is closed off to yourself, and it is closed off to others. For example, before I felt safe sharing my emotions with God, I struggled to identify and articulate how I felt to myself and others. So, my default was always to shut down in fear or as a sign of passive resistance. This was the next level that God addressed.

One night, the guy and I got into one of the stupidest fights in history. We spent so much time talking to each other that we neglected key responsibilities. I knew it, and he knew it. But he was the only one brave enough to raise the issue and ask that we set some structure around our interactions so we could spend time together without neglecting our personal goals.

It was a reasonable request that I agreed with. But how he raised the matter and what he said caused my fear of abandonment and rejection to rear its ugly head. Instead of sharing my fears, agreeing with his approach, or proposing an approach that allayed my worries, I shut down. I told him it was fine if he needed space because I also needed space to catch up with my other friends who I had neglected. My response pissed him off, and he grew distant. See? I told you, stupidest fight in history.

His behaviour persisted into the night and all the following day despite several manipulative attempts on my part to jerk him out of his feelings. Later that evening, after barely speaking the entire day, he called. He kept the conversation brief. I went from feeling sorry for hurting him to straight-out pissed off. In my mind, he was being totally unreasonable and confusing. I was legit in "damn him to hell" and "he can take a long jump off a short bridge" mad mode. I wanted to punish him for being a jackass. I was so angry I needed a nap to cool off.

As I waited to doze off, I scrolled mindlessly on Pinterest. I paused only when I came across an image referring to 1 Corinthians 13 with the following words:

My mom always told me to replace the word 'love' with my man's name, and if it's not accurate, he's not the one.

1 Corinthians 13:4-7 **New International Version (NIV)**

4 Love is patient, love is kind. It does not envy, it does not boast, it is not proud.

5 It does not dishonour others, it is not self-seeking, it is not easily angered, it keeps no record of wrongs.

6 Love does not delight in evil but rejoices with the truth.

7 It always protects, always trusts, always hopes, always perseveres.

Intoxicated with self-righteousness, I plugged in his name and rejoiced when it turned out I was right. He wasn't displaying any of these characteristics. I couldn't wait to tell on him to my Father, but first, I needed that nap.

When I woke, I immediately stepped into my time with God. I launched into my story, heavy on the blame game.

"See God! He is not displaying all the characteristics of love, and I want him punished!"

"But neither are you," God gently chided. "If you plug your name in, you'll come up short as well."

Sally say what?! My brain short-circuited. I calmed right down, the wind fully knocked out of my blaming sails. I hated to admit it, but God was right. I was not being patient. I wasn't being kind. I was being proud, thinking he was the only one with "issues." I was being irritable and was ready to demand my own way. I was certainly not enduring. In essence, I was being anything but loving, and we both had lost total sight of the issue at hand.

"Oh, my God! I have totally messed up. He's not even talking to me. Lord, what do I do?"

Let me tell you something. When you ask God for solutions, be prepared to either get the "foolishness" that will confound the wise or steps that will take you out of your comfort zone. Do you know what He told me? He said I should acknowledge that I too was in the wrong and apologize. Since all my "comfortable" strategies had failed, I decided I had nothing to lose by trying God's way. To say I was terrified is very tame. I was petrified! Shamefaced, I asked for the words to say and found myself inspired to write a letter that included "I love you." My thumbs hovered over the "I love you" and deleted and retyped it many times before I threw caution to the wind and hit send before putting the phone on silent and tossing it to the side like hot bread.

Minutes later, I peeked over at it and noticed the flickering green light signalling a new notification. My heart was in my mouth. I fought between the desire to ignore the phone and pick it up. Pick it up won. Heart pounding, I pressed the power button, and the phone lit up to show a response from him. I tapped in my passcode and clicked the email open to a response and change in behaviour that made me cry. All anger was gone and transgressions forgiven, "I love you too."

That moment proved to be the trigger for the domino effect I never realized I needed. My tongue loosened, and I found myself sharing more of my feelings, not just with the guy but also with my friends.

Though still tentative in many areas, I found myself sharing my story more and more. It drew others to me, and I got a glimpse of the impact I could have. I experienced the wonder of truly sharing with both friends and strangers, and I love it. I caught a glimpse of how people could experience freedom and healing through my willingness to stand up, speak up, and own the wisdom and experiences that God had given me. It was a small glimpse, but it opened my eyes to the possibilities and whetted my appetite for more.

Sometimes you may not know what to do with yourself after you experience the wonder of expressing your emotions, especially when everyone else in your life is used to you suppressing your emotions. It gets even more complicated when everyone at home handles their emotions in the old way. That was me with my mother and family. Our family legacy and culture were built on never being emotional or sharing our emotions. We showed that we cared through provision, and that was it.

When my eyes opened and I experienced the wonder of my vulnerability, I saw the legacy my family had successfully passed to my siblings and me. It was evident between my grandmother and her kids. I decided in my heart that it would stop with me. It wouldn't be something I passed on to my children. I broke the chains of a generational curse when I hugged my mother for the first time at twenty-eight and told her that I loved her. She looked at me as though I had grown two heads. She didn't say a word, but it was one of the most freeing moments I've ever felt in my life. I purposed in my heart to say it more to her. This was one of those moments where change started with me.

As a teenager, one of my favourite songs was *Big Girls Don't Cry.* Fergie lied to herself and us. Big girls do cry, and it's quite okay. Another mantra I heeded was, "Put some dirt in it, and smile because it could be worse." Yes, it could be worse, and when life gives me lemons, I should see the opportunities to make lemonade, but that doesn't mean I have to stop being human.

God doesn't expect us to stop being human or bottle up our emotions. Instead, he longs for us to recognize that He is our safe space and that He can lead us to share with others. In the words of Gospel singer Chandler Moore, God wants us to know that "It's okay to not be okay. Love leaves room for you to say, 'I'm not okay ....' There ain't no shame in letting go." When you accept this truth, it transforms your relationship with God, yourself, and others. It even opens the doors for you to minister to others and impact lives just by sharing you authentically. When you get to that stage, you begin to recognize that Love leaves room for you to be who God has called you to be and have massive impact. But before you can walk fully into that, you'll have one enormous monster to face.

REFLECTION

Let's make God the Safe Space for your emotions. What is stopping you from trusting Him and others with your emotions?

9

THE ME GOD SEES

A three-year-old boy walks into the living room and turns to proudly display his shirt to his father who is sitting on the couch. The shirt read, "My dad is a total legend." The father laughs uproariously.

"Wow, Judah! I didn't know your dad was a legend. Are you a legend too?"

The son pauses, his forehead furrowed as he contemplates his answer.

"No, I'm not a legend. I'm Judah Keto," he declares proudly. "That is my name!"

Even at three, Judah knew and owned his identity.

Many of us are nothing like young Judah: we let the world label us. The circumstances we were born in, others' expectations, culture, and the issues of life beat our identity and self-esteem bloody. Every time it tried to rise up, it was pounded back into the ground by the thumps of heavy iron fists.

That was my story. After a while, my identity and self-esteem stopped fighting against everything that life threw at me. As life planted its muddied boots on its back and roared triumphantly, my self-esteem lay face-down in the dirt and learned to cope with the new identity that life had decided was its portion. I became a high-performing perfectionist with a tendency for control. I told everybody that I was a child of God, but they were just words, nothing else. But the time was coming for a change. It came in a way I least expected.

THE AGITATOR

The night when my mind checked out briefly, it affected me deeply. It fanned the flames of an already roaring desire for purpose into an unquenchable monster that consumed everything in its path. I could no longer hide behind my excuses or pretend that everything was okay when it wasn't. My desire to discover my purpose wouldn't let me.

I wore my mask for a few months more, but dissatisfaction clamoured at me. The need for more beat at my door. The need to be more weighed heavily on my heart, and I questioned God constantly about my purpose. I struggled to deal with the war that raged within my heart as the need to release myself from the tight grips of the control I'd mastered steamrolled over me constantly. *There had to be more to life than this.*

The measures of success I had previously clung to no longer gave me peace. I hated to admit it, but at what many would consider the height of my career, I was the unhappiest and most dissatisfied I had ever been. I wanted more but had no idea where to start or how to get it, especially when I thought of all the responsibilities I had in my life. Then things shifted without me realising it. It all started with a strong urge to leave my corporate job.

THE BEHAVIOURAL RESPONSE

I immediately rejected the idea of leaving my job. There was no way I could do it. For almost all my life, I had controlled how I was seen to avoid ridicule and criticism. I was born to fit in and had worked hard to find a world where I lived up to that expectation. I had spent my whole life mastering the art of being Luisa Madrigal, the strongest child in the movie *Encanto* whose gift of strength could always be relied upon to carry the burdens of the Madrigal family. I was the strong one who did what I was told and carried the burdens without complaining or considering my needs too deeply. I had mastered Isabela Madrigal's perfectionistic tendencies. Nothing was ever out of place. Any frustration was always hidden by a smile or cast to the back of my mind to be dealt with later. Like Isabela, who almost married a man she didn't love, I was even willing to sacrifice myself in relationships I didn't want if that was what others needed.

I was the good daughter who had followed the path that everyone expected of the smart Christian one. I had done well in primary and high school. I'd gone on to college, by the grace of God, without my mom having to worry about tuition. Then I found a good job and worked my ass off to get to where I was. I even had all the degrees and certifications and the admiration and praises of my peers to prove that I was good – extremely good – at what I do. Now, I was getting this urge to walk away from all of that?

How then was I feeling the urge to be like Mirabel Madrigal? I couldn't be the sore thumb, the one who didn't fit anyone's expectations. It didn't matter if I was dissatisfied. It didn't matter if my true self begged daily for a chance to be seen. Hiding was survival; fitting in was survival, and I wanted nothing more than to survive. There was no way I was even going to consider undertaking this mission, much less without some kind of firm backup plan.

THE VALID NEED

For the majority of my life, I felt like the ugly duckling. I didn't fit in well, so I searched for a place where I felt secure and accepted. I longed to be affirmed in who I was and feel like I belonged. It didn't matter the place or with whom. I wanted a sense of security and acceptance with my family, friends, at work, at church and within myself. When I thought I had found it, even if it hurt to hang on, I held on for dear life because I firmly believed that life wouldn't get any better than that.

I also didn't know who I was outside the worlds I had created. My identity hinged on my job role, so I held on for dear life. I improved myself daily to climb the corporate ladder and prove I was good because if I lost that role and identity, I didn't know who I'd be. My identity belonged to everyone but me. It was tied to the close friends I had. I became possessive and jealous if they made space for others because I saw that as a threat to our relationship. My identity was tied to being an Apostolic Christian, so I played the part to a T, even if that meant ignoring the questions I had and stifling my inner voice that clamoured for release. The worlds I fit in weren't perfect, but I belonged, at least to the external eye. But it was a belonging I would fight tooth and nail to keep.

THE TRAUMA EVENT

I used to be an outgoing, extroverted tomboy who loved hanging with my brother and his friends. We lived the glorious life of typical Jamaican 90's babies. We climbed trees, jumped down into gullies to retrieve fruits, or, just for the heck of it, played cricket and drove box trucks throughout the countryside. For a young girl who worshipped her older brother, it was exhilarating, drops, bruises and all.

My sexual molestation at the age of six changed everything for me. I didn't realise just how much I lost until I came across a quote from an interview with Maya Angelou and Bill Moyers [1] about facing evil. Maya discussed how her childhood rape turned into her love of reading, poetry, and literature. She stated: "Rape on the body of a young person, more often than not, introduces cynicism, and there is nothing quite so tragic as a young cynic. Because it means that the person has gone from knowing nothing to believing nothing." I was so surprised the first time I came across that quote! It impacted me in so many ways. I recalled my unjustified amounts of cynicism as a preteen and teenager. As a survivor of childhood sexual assault, I understood the story – no, I *felt* the story. I laid my own story on top of hers and saw the parallels.

I, too, lost my physical voice and the voice of my essence. I lost me. I never spoke of what happened to me until I was almost thirty. I became a cynic, and I did not trust people. I found it hard to receive from others because I always wondered what strings were attached to the gift. I did not believe there was anything good or beautiful or worthwhile outside of what I could control. In fact, I was too scared to care about much of anything.

After my sexual abuse, I shifted into a more reserved and introverted version of my formerly outgoing self. I could not risk standing out too much from the crowd or doing something that would make me be chosen for some vile act again. So I kept my mouth shut and stuck my nose in my books. I had an affinity for women like Beatrice, from Shakespeare's *Much Ado About Nothing*, who bested Benedict with her wit, and Portia from *The Merchant of Venice* who saved a friend's life by outwitting the Jewish moneylender Shylock who demanded a pound of flesh. I was inspired by women from the Bible like Deborah, the first female judge of Israel, Abigail, whose bravery and wisdom prevented the death of her household despite her husband's foolishness. And Queen Esther who, despite the circumstances, allowed God to use her to save her people. I wanted to be like these women. I wanted to be like Mulan, the Disney princess who didn't fit in but became the unexpected heroine who saved China from the Huns. I loved that each of these women owned their voice, and I wanted to be like them, but I just couldn't.

Hiding was survival. In hiding, I began to stand out in a different way. My love for books and my reserved nature earned me the label "nerd" from my family. I struggled to connect with my siblings and became the brunt of the joke whenever they realised that I couldn't do something or didn't know a pop culture reference or something they thought the dumbest person should know. "Yuh so smart and don't know that?" Or "How yuh have college degree and don't know that?" Peals of laughter would follow. I crept deeper into my shell, ashamed, and resolved to say nothing unless I was certain of the answer and do nothing unless I could do it perfectly. By the time I reached high school, I was a tight bundle of control, but even then, I wasn't safe. There were still nails to be pounded into my coffin. The nails were situations designed to push me over the edge into timidity by taking whatever was left of the voice that channelled my purpose.

I had a knack for writing and directing skits. I would get an idea, write the parts, and then organise everything and everyone into place. My shame came when I decided to dance and speak patois before a class full of teenagers, though I wasn't good at it. No one remembered my orchestration brilliance. Instead, they all zoned on weakness, my far from perfect ability to dance to rhythms and properly speak the patios of my island home. Heat burned the cheeks of my brown skin as I became the laughingstock before a classroom of thirty-eight kids. I resolved then and there that I would never be laughed at or ridiculed by anyone in private or public. Being different or standing out was a shame and burden I couldn't bear. I was not built for it.

And so, I was reborn, except I was timid and voiceless. I was the girl who held tightly to the reins that control afforded me. I did not speak up about anything. When I tried, my insides quivered, and I'd step back shakily into the comfort and safety that silence and timidity offered. I didn't take chances. I had to be certain and have everything planned out to the T. I valued perfectionism and took pride in my performance. I even took to pretending that I was high and mighty and that my lifestyle was way better than it actually was. I mastered the art of copying others around me to ensure I fit in so well that I was least likely to be singled out.

THE LIE I BELIEVED

One night as I listened to a podcast episode by Susan Fleming, a Business Alignment Therapist who equips Kingdom leadership to multiply LIFE – legacy, impact, freedom, energy – without burnout, she asked listeners to do something strange.

"Write down the immediate thoughts that came to your mind when you think about yourself and money."

After a few moments of contemplation, I wrote down the following:

- I am not enough.
- People will hire me, and I will fail them.
- I have to work hard to get money.
- I am not worthy to be in the room. I am a nobody.
- I don't know enough. I am a fake.
- I shouldn't call attention to myself.
- Nobody will buy from me.

GOD'S TRUTH

To say I was shocked by the gravity of what I had written down was the understatement of the year! I stopped the podcast and immediately went before God and cried my eyes out over the junky thoughts about myself that I had been walking around with unsuspectingly.

God gave me one scripture:

"For God is working in you, giving you the desire and the power to do what pleases him." - Philippians 2:13

He then reminded me of the exercise He made me do years earlier where I rewrote the statements into truths and promises He had told me. I wrote down the following and began declaring them over myself.

- The Holy Spirit lives in me, so I am more than enough. I was made in His image.
- God has equipped me with everything I need to serve well. I can do all things through Christ who strengthens me.
- I am never in lack. I don't need to work hard to be rich. Wealth is my inheritance. God has given me the power to create wealth. Money serves me. I have dominion over it. I have access to all the resources He has given to me.
- I am God's (the King's) daughter. I am of a royal priesthood. I belong wherever He puts me. My name will be called in rooms I don't know of. I will go before kings.
- I am exactly where I am called to be and fully equipped for my calling. I have everything I need.
- I am called to impact and influence millions. It's not

about pride. I'm representing Christ. I'm doing it for
His Glory.

- It's God's business, and His purpose for it will be
  fulfilled.

WHAT DID GOD TELL ME TO DO?

God had other plans for me. Though I longed for it to be otherwise, He had given me a voice and a purpose. It was one that didn't belong in the graveyard I would have gladly relegated it to.

In my second year of high school, one of my favourite teachers asked a question during our study of Shakespeare's *The Merchant of Venice*. I muttered my opinion as she waited for the answers, not expecting her to hear. But she did. She asked me a few times what I had said, but terrified, I remained mute. Disappointment shadowed her eyes as she went on to reveal the correct answer to her question. It was the one I had refused to say out loud to the class. She would go on to share the incident and express her disappointment to my mom at the next parent-teacher conference.

She cautioned me about my behaviour and urged me to speak up. It was a caution that I ignored for the majority of my life, even though I tended to be forced into leadership roles or roles that required my voice. I shied away as much as possible, hiding behind managers and occasionally pretending to be sick so I could get out of it. But I could only do that for so long. As months went by, the persistent clamouring to leave my job increased in my ear. I ignored it. Finally, in an attempt to shut it up, I started applying for jobs here and there. I got interviews, but they either ended up not being a good fit for me or me for them. I took that as a sign that I wasn't meant to leave just yet and shifted back into the rise and grind of the average corporate life.

I asked God about purpose as it related to my job.

"I've never done things the way you expected," He said. "Your job won't come in the manner you expect it."

When I pressed Him, He continued.

"I will give you a job that aligns with your purpose and makes you excited each day. However, there are things you need to come to terms with. If I revealed it to you now, when you are not ready, you would reject it."

Man, was He right! He didn't show me the full picture then, but He began to shift me. Things took a turn when I started getting sick often. I recognised the signs of what I knew was my body's way of warning me of my impending burnout. I prayed about it, and God said one word "Leave." I resigned a few days later with no solid plan in place. I had two part-time virtual assistant clients and only three months of savings in my bank account.

THE PROCESS TO FREEDOM

We make plans, but God laughs because our ways are definitely not His ways. I can just imagine the belly-clutching laughter that erupted from His throat when He heard my plans to become a virtual assistant. He didn't stop me from going after it, but I soon realised I was meant for bigger things. The journey I started was leading straight to releasing control to God and accepting my identity in Him.

I spent half of my savings within five days of leaving corporate. I knew I couldn't start a serious virtual assistant business on my own. I needed help, so when a coach landed in my lap, I signed up by faith. It didn't work out, but I caught a glimpse of a bigger problem in the business industry. Many coaches, consultants, and experts really wanted to help their clients get results but were going about it all wrong. It was a way that led to little results and burnout or consistent results with burnout. I had my own David moment when he heard Goliath mocking Israel and God. But there was one difference between David and me; I saw the problem clearly, and it frustrated me, but it didn't even cross my mind that I could do something about it. It was someone else's problem.

I held on tightly to what I thought I knew about myself and how far I could go. Even when God moved on my heart about the problem He had shown to me, I refused to accept and step fully into the role He wanted me to take. *I wasn't good enough to do that. I didn't have the necessary skills. God, are you crazy?* were the lines of conversation that I had with Him frequently. I accepted that He had delivered me from the Egypt experience of the corporate world and wanted me in my own business, but my mind had not yet experienced freedom. I was stuck on what I *thought* was possible. I was caught up in what I could see and control. I also took suggestions from way too many people and looked everywhere to find people I could copy and tried to do what they were doing. It was no surprise that none of that worked, and what I was doing became a convoluted mess that even I could no longer see clearly through.

The results were delayed because God could not have that fractured version of me do the vision's work. The wrestling between my world-given and God-given identities needed to end. He had called me to greater, and He needed me to understand that and trust that He – not me or others – had the full plan and knew the path I needed to take.

One morning at about 3:00am, He woke me up. He played out in my mind my career lifeline and showed me how all my experiences up to that moment had prepared me for this. I was created for such a time as this. My knack for seeing the bigger picture and breaking it down into step-by-step quantifiable pieces was needed for such a time as this. My people-focused approach to serving and all my previous work projects were vital to the mission He had called me to. My tendency to find a way to make progress measurable was exactly what was needed for such a time as this. Everything was leading up to me stepping into business.

"Chanel, you were created for this. Stop doubting yourself and step out."

For the first time, I believed Him. I could solve the problem I felt led to solve through my business. I had already done it in many different shapes and forms throughout my career. But I still had one hurdle to face. Though I had evidence that I could do it, I still held on to my limits. I struggled to trust God and cede my control in favour of His plan.

The following month, God broke me and established my faith in Him in the most unexpected way. I ran out of money. I looked at both my bank accounts and saw only 500 Jamaican dollars in both. For context, that was less than ten United States dollars. As I sat on my couch that Friday evening and gazed at my computer screen, indignation rose up in me, and I challenged God.

"God, I don't like this. I haven't seen my accounts this low in years. You put me here, and You better do something about this."

That was the first time since I began my journey that I accepted that things were out of my control. This was way bigger than me, and none of my plans could work. God had to fix this, and I truly believed in my heart that He would not bring me to shame. He was going to come through on time.

The following Monday, as I did some client work, I felt a strong compulsion to check my bank account. I kept working and eventually forgot. Later that week, I heard a prompting.

"Chanel, check your account."

Curious, I logged into the banking portal and, to my surprise, I found money waiting. I was puzzled because it wasn't expected. When I investigated further, I realised a client had paid me far in advance for work I was contracted to do. The amount would cover all my expenses for the following month. He did come through, much earlier than I expected, and in a way that brought tears to my eyes and cemented my faith in Him.

That experience gave me huge insight into who God is. God is a Master Planner and Orchestrator, and each of us has a significant role to play in His big plan. As a former project manager, I was responsible for all the project plans and implementation. I always knew what was coming up because it was my job to know. Even if my team forgot that we had planned all the steps together, I had to know everything about the project and ensure we got results. I even handled all the issues and risks.

Similar to the work I did, that's how God manages the entire world and is always a million steps ahead. He has all the pieces and knows who needs to do what and how everything is connected. He accounted for every step that we need to take and when. He accounted for every risk and issue we could encounter along these steps. He is also aware of all the decisions we need to make and when each person needs to come into play. He is coordinating all that and has accounted for it all!

While we only have the capacity for plan A to Z, He has the capacity for infinite plans of action, not that He ever needed them. And whilst we fall asleep on the job, He is always awake and watching, ready to catch us when we fall and help us get back on track. For the first time ever, it hit me that He was the best "man" for the job of being in control of my life. He was equipped to keep me safe and secure. All He needed was for me to stop trying to take control and let Him show me the little piece that I needed to take. It's His responsibility to figure out how it would work and when. The weight of responsibility and control lifted from my shoulders, and I handed it fully over to Him, allowing Him to flex my faith muscles and obedience more.

Once I handed over the reins, I gave God permission to take me on a path that would shift how I saw myself. He tuned my ears and spirit to those around me. I realised that I struggled terribly with fear because the spirit of timidity and cautiousness had taken up residence in my lineage. When I listened to my mom talk, *"be timid"* was all I heard. *Don't do this because it will turn out badly. Stick to what is known and comfortable, and stay far from the unknown. The unknown hurts.* That was the pattern I heard all day long, so it was no wonder that my subconscious believed that mantra. It was no wonder my subconscious rebelled heavily whenever God tried to take me from the shore and out into the deep; that's where my purpose waited for me with wide open arms.

I decided that fear would not be my future. It shouldn't be anybody's future when our Father knows everything about tomorrow and tells us not to worry about tomorrow because it will take care of itself. I didn't need to be bold; I just needed to trust God. I didn't need to be brave or a legend. I just needed to know that I am Chanel Robe, the daughter of the Most High God who cares deeply for His children. He already validated me. He is where all of my Help comes from, and He has already given me all I need to step fully into what He has called me to. So, I stepped out into business and life and did what God told me. I owned my passion for helping individuals and entrepreneurs serve people without overwhelm and burnout. I owned that I had everything I needed to win in life and in business. And even though it was scary, I owned my voice and shared what was on my heart with the world. For the first time in a long time, I felt a wave of satisfaction, anticipation, and excitement about the future.

Someone once asked me where I got my resources for my future plans. My response was simple: "I'm partnering with God, so whilst I don't know, He does, and so I'm not worried about it." When we hold on to control, we choose our plans over God's plans, and that conflict puts a lot of responsibility on our shoulders to make "it" happen. However, when you stick with God's plan, He'll take you on an adventure that you never expected to take, one that goes exceedingly abundantly above all the things we could ever think, dare to dream or imagine.

Suddenly, exceedingly abundant shifts from just getting the desires of your heart to getting that and all the things you didn't even know you needed. You get to show up with your God-given voice without the pressure of making results happen. You get peace and joy. You get deliverance from needing external validation. You get access to a never-ending boost of faith. You get freed from generational curses. You get delivered from sins that held you captive for a lifetime. You get better relationships with others. You see you better and fall in love with yourself all over again.

That's the beauty of handing over the reins of control to God. Of course, it doesn't mean that sometimes you won't try to take it back. But you give Him permission to take you on the path He always had planned for you. It's a path you would have never imagined in your wildest dreams and one I'm waiting to see unfold as you own your God-given voice. But it only comes when you show up fully as you and partner with God to make it happen.

REFLECTION

Let's give God control over your life. What is stopping you from giving Him the reins?

____
____
____
____
____
____
____
____
____
____
____
____
____
____
____
____
____
____

Let's give God control over your life. What is stopping you from giving Him the reins?

PART III

You say I am loved when I can't feel a thing
You say I am strong when I think I am weak
And you say I am held when I am falling short
And when I don't belong, oh You say I am Yours
And I believe. What You say of me.
The only thing that matters now is everything You think of me.
In You I find my worth; in You I find my identity.

– Lauren Daigle

10

FLAMINGO PINK

"Chanel …"

"Hmmmn?"

"You're like a pink flamingo."

"Yeah, yeah," I mumbled as I fanned away the comment. I fell back into a light doze.

I don't know about you, but while I love God's revelations, I'm not the biggest fan of being awakened at 5:00am on a Sunday morning by anyone, even God. Plus, I don't like pink.

A few hours later, my eyes opened, and I made a beeline line to my computer to jot down a new idea.

I lifted the laptop lid to reveal a screen full of flamingos. The comment that God had made before flashed across my mind. It seemed He had a point He really wanted to make.

"Have you ever wondered why of all the colours, flamingos are pink?"

"Nooo," I mused.

"Pink is a bright colour. They are so pink that you can't miss them. That's what I meant when I said you are like a flamingo. You have the flamingo pinkness that is uniquely you. You cannot hide."

It was an interesting thought to ponder, but He definitely made sense. It explained why even though I tried to hide, like King Saul who was too tall to hide behind a pile of baggage, I was always the obvious choice. I ran from leadership, but leadership came running after me. Heck, most of the time I ended up leading people who were forty and fifty years older than me! I ran from advising anyone, but even CEOs sought me out for advice.

The Lord had my attention but fleetingly. I eventually forgot about this early morning epiphany. As I wrote this book, He brought it back to me, and I looked up what a flamingo represents. The word that stood out to me the most was 'confidence.'

What God had tried to tell me before hit me afresh. Being uniquely you, being the flamingo you, takes confidence. It requires that you not be so well-adjusted to your culture that you fit in without even thinking. And when I talk about culture, I'm referring to your home life, work life, church life, you name it. Being uniquely you requires you to live on this earth but not automatically accept its values, even the ones you inherit. It requires you to not copy others and try to be a nose when you were called to be and carry out the essential purpose of the armpits. It requires you to stand confidently in the form of who you are called to be and own your voice: own you, your gifts and your purpose and calling.

I love this quote from Pastor Robert Madu's *Confidence Under Pressure* sermon: "The enemy cannot touch your gift. He cannot touch your call. Oh, but he can definitely touch your confidence. And he will attack your confidence because if he can get your confidence, you will shrink away from your call, deny the gift that is in you, buckle under the pressure, and fear will stop you from stepping out." That's how he steals your voice. He uses the winds and waves of your life to trick you into throwing away your confidence so that you step out of alignment with God and miss what God has promised (Hebrews 10:35-36).

Sometimes, if you are anything like I was, you'll look like you have it all together on the outside, but the reality is that you are paddling like hell to keep afloat by your own strength. The enemy and your ego tricked you into missing the joy, peace, safety, comfort, and blessings to be found in being in an amazing relationship with Christ. They tricked you into missing the blessing of showing up as your true flamingo self, flaws and all, and seeing the impact it has on the lives of those around you. He tricked you into missing the blessing of deeper intimacy that comes from heart-to-heart relationships with the people who mean the most to you.

Today, it is time to say "No more!" to the lies that the enemy and your ego tricked you into believing about God, yourself, and the people around you. It is time you stop missing out on God's promises for your life. It's time for your heart and mind to accept God's truth and the identity and purpose that He carved out for you before you were in your mother's womb. It is time to own all of your true flamingo-pink voice. Your voice is valuable. You are valuable. Your purpose and calling are valuable.

You may be worried that you will be humiliated or, worse yet, killed for daring to be yourself and going into spaces where you haven't been invited, but God placed you here and now for such a time as this. You have the exact position and level of authority you need to do what He called you to do.

You may have a disability or impediment that makes you self-conscious. You believe that you are not usable but know that God has a bigger plan that is custom-made for you. He already considered your disability or impediment and still chose you. You are His choice. He does not want to send anyone else on this assignment.

You may feel like you are the least qualified. You may believe you don't come from the right family or background or don't have the right degrees or experiences. You feel like a nobody. But know one thing. God doesn't always call the qualified. But He does qualify whomever He calls. Believe that He is your strength in the areas where you are weak.

You may be hiding because you believe God chose wrong, that you're not cut out for what God is calling you to do, but that's not true. Your voice is a perfect fit, even if people despise your appointment.

No matter what you believe, you are here for such a time as this. The Master Planner did the math and determined that this is the season when your voice will be most needed. There are problems on the earth that you have been equipped with the specific gifts, skills, and experiences to solve. There are people your flamingo-pink voice is meant to heal, deliver, impact and influence.

So, do not let the rules of culture and this world silence you. Own your voice and ask for what you want. The future of other women and their children's children depend on it.

I would be remiss if I ended here without sharing with you some strategies you can use daily to own your voice and avoid falling into the trap of living only to meet others' expectations.

GO DEEPER WITH GOD

Make God your top priority, and spend time with Him. When I say spend time, I don't just mean having that set structure where you sit each day, read your bible, pray, and then go on your way. Make room for God in your time with Him. Make time to listen to His voice because prayer is a conversation and is not just you talking, talking and talking some more. It's good to have a structure, but don't be so rigid that God has no room to move and shift the order.

Do not neglect to go deep. Shift from a surface relationship where you pray for everyone but yourself. Open up your heart to Him and share your worries and cares. Share your joys and heartbreaks. Share anything and everything with Him as you would your best friend at any minute of the day.

Gospel singer Chandler Moore said something that I've never forgotten "When you start to see God, you start to see you." This is quite true. Deeper time with God transforms you and purifies the desires of your heart to align with His will for your life. You start to see your insecurities. You start to get agitated and uncover lies that the enemy has told you, and you believed. It shifts you inside out. It makes you see you and evokes a humbleness that causes you to see and face up to the truth quicker. I cannot tell you how many times I shifted from anger, indignation and self-righteousness to apologetic and peacemaker because I sat down with God and He showed me me.

Deeper relationship with God makes you more vulnerable and sensitive to yourself and others and His voice in every area of your daily life. Imagine being so sensitive to God that you hear His directions clearly as you go about your day-to-day business!

Deeper relationship with God opens your eyes to the ways He has fought and continues to fight for you. It builds the level of trust and security that comes with the confidence that you don't have to worry because He is quite capable of handling the cares that you give to Him, and He already took care of tomorrow. So, my dear flamingo, stop skating on the surface. Go deeper with God.

TUNE YOUR EAR AND MAKE GOD YOUR GPS

Once you go deeper with God, you will hear and recognize His voice more often. Don't let the worries, cares or busyness of your life cause you to miss His voice. Tune your ear to Him and make Christ your GPS. Don't lean on your own understanding or the opinions or advice of others. Your interpretation of things is often fuelled by your own biases and assumptions. And though well-meaning, some people will advise you from a place of fear. Some will speak over you from the position of their own perceived limits. Even though some may have some expertise, they do not know the full picture of what God intended for you.

So, when you tune your ear to everyone but God, it slows you down, shifts you into trying to meet the expectations of others and confuses you to the point where you struggle to own your voice and know which direction to go. Instead of going around in circles trying to get understanding from everyone, ask God for wisdom and the right advisors. Only God has the blueprint for your life. Ask Him for directions and trust Him even if His instructions mean going against the grain. You'll be in for the ride of your life on a journey that brings forth exceeding abundance. So, my dear flamingo, stop relying solely on the opinion of others. Make God your GPS.

TRUST GOD WITH YOUR ONE AND ONLY

It is hard to release control to God when you believe you only have one shot. What you see is not what God sees. For example, God promised Abraham that he would be the father of many nations, although he had no heirs in his old age. Over time, Abraham had two sons, yet God told him that it was okay to send away Ishmael and then asked Abraham to sacrifice Isaac. That would literally put Abraham back at square one: no heirs and no way to fulfil the promise that God gave him.

If I was Abraham, I would have had a "what the hell?!" moment and told God no. But not Abraham. God had his heart and his 'yes' even when it meant that what he could now see did not in any way line up with what God had promised him. Abraham did not withhold from God his one and only, the thing he deemed most precious and saw as the thing God would use to fulfil His promise to him.

Abraham's blessing came because he showed God that He was the top priority in his heart and trusted that God was in control and would keep his promise. So, my dear flamingo, don't be a control hoarder. Be an Abraham, and hand over the controls and trust God with your one and only.

SHIFT YOUR FOCUS

Focus on the things you are gaining. Don't miss the blessing because you are focused on all the things you are losing. Signs of God's favour are there even in the midst of your loss.

Don't be like Leah who was unhappy for years because she focused on the wrong thing. She focused on the love and approval that her husband did not give her and missed God's favour in locking her rival's womb and blessing her with four sons. It wasn't until her fourth son that Leah shifted her attention from seeking external approval to acknowledging God's blessing and praising Him. Imagine how much peace, joy and love she missed out on because of where she had focused.

Let me be honest with you about one more thing. When you get into a deeper relationship with Christ and begin to show up in your flamingo pinkness, God will strip you. He is going to empty you out in some areas of your life. But know that there is a reason for your "empty boat." For example, Peter, James, and John's empty boat provided an opportunity for God to step in, minister to them and others, convert them and change the course of their lives. My empty bank account was an opportunity for God to show that He had everything under control. He needs to empty you of all the stuff before He fills you up. I wouldn't be where I am today without the many empty boat seasons that I endured. So, my dear flamingo, don't miss the blessing in your empty boat. Shift your focus.

PROGRESSION, NOT PERFECTION

Despite our intentions, things won't always go as we planned. We will mess up. Paul had a thorn in his flesh that he wrestled with daily. David messed up, yet God still saw fit to declare him a man after His heart. Abraham went ahead of God and got Hagar pregnant with Ishmael, but he is still known today as a man of great faith. Your mess up does not have to be where your story ends.

It's about progression, not perfection. Recognize that God's love comes with a healthy dose of grace, so don't beat yourself up. Don't hide away from Him in shame or blame others like Adam and Eve did after eating the forbidden fruit in the Garden of Eden. Like the father who waited for his prodigal son to return home, God is ready and able to offer you compassion and forgiveness and restore you to your formerly rejected position as a beloved son or daughter. All He needs is your repentance.

So, my dear flamingo, progress daily alongside Him and be kind to yourself. And with that said, I must add one more thing. Do you know the Lord hates when we "condemn the innocent?" That's straight from Proverbs 17:15. That means He hates when your inner critic takes a whip to your mental and emotional back. He hates when you constantly find fault with, berate, or criticize yourself. So give grace to yourself and others. I mention others because the same measure you give to others is the same measure that will be given to you. So, be kind to yourself and others. Remember, progression, not perfection.

BE YOURSELF

My amazing flamingo, you are made in God's image. Sin and life may have made you rough around the edges, but God longs for you to show up daily as who He called you to be, even as He refines you. The world needs you in all your flamingo pinkness. So, forget dancing like nobody is watching. Dance like a toddler. They don't even care if there is music. Show up as your full flamingo-pink self, scars, feelings, and all. Get off the sidelines of your life despite the fear that tells you it is safer there. Kick timidity to the curb and show up boldly to your calling.

Don't worry about what everyone will think or what they expect. In the words of God to me, "Looking at life through those lenses has more to do with your pride and self-importance. Nobody is that caught up in everything you do. And even if they are, it shouldn't matter anyway as long as you are in alignment with Me." Jesus taught us one key thing: you can be the most innocent person alive, and people will still find a reason to hate or dislike you. Don't let it bother you. Not everyone will understand your journey, and that's okay. Don't let it stop you from showing up in your full flamingo pinkness. Own your voice and your weirdness fully.

Comparison to others is definitely unwelcome. Even if someone else is doing it, your pink flamingo voice makes the difference and changes the game. See others as inspirations, not competition. If God can use them to do that, imagine what He can use you to do.

Instead of focusing on all the reasons you can't own and show the world your voice, think of all the reasons you should. Imagine the impact, influence, and exceeding abundance that God has called you to. Imagine the amazing relationships you can have with God, others, and yourself. Imagine what you and the world would miss out on if you rejected your purpose and calling. Just imagine!

Even as you imagine, know one thing: God's will *will* be done on Earth with or without you. None of us can hold God hostage by refusing to show up. When King Saul stopped playing his assigned role and stepped out of alignment with God, there was a David waiting in the wings. So, ponder and imagine but don't let God have to find a David to do what He called you to do and be. My dear flamingo, kick others' expectations and your timidity and fear to the curb. Own your flamingo-pink voice and show up fully in the purpose God has called you to.

REFLECTION

Let's get you owning your flamingo-pink voice.

STEP ONE: Write down the immediate thoughts that come to mind when you think about yourself.

____

____

____

____

____

____

____

____

____

____

____

____

____

____

____

____

____

____

STEP TWO: Now focus your thoughts on how God sees you and who He has called you to be. Write down what God and the Bible say about each of the thoughts you wrote down.

____

____

____

____

____

____

____

____

____

____

____

____

____

____

____

____

____

____

STEP THREE: Pause daily. Look at yourself in the mirror and remind yourself of those truths.

SELF-EXPLORATION

STEP ONE: RAISE YOUR AWARENESS

THE AGITATOR

Write down a one-off moment, recurring problem, or event that triggers you immensely.

____

____

____

____

____

____

____

____

____

____

____

____

____

____

THE BEHAVIOURAL RESPONSE

Write down how you reacted to the problem, event, or moment that occurred.

THE VALID NEED

Write down why you reacted that way? Which of your needs wasn't being fulfilled at that moment?

STEP TWO: DIG DEEPER. ASK THE LORD WHY YOU EXPERIENCE THAT PATTERN.

THE TRAUMA EVENT

Write down what the Lord shows you about the root cause of the pattern started and how it affected you.

____

____

____

____

____

____

____

____

____

____

____

____

____

____

____

THE LIE I BELIEVED

Write down the lie you believed or the vow you made to deal with the effects of the trauma event.

GOD'S TRUTH

Write down what God and the Bible say about your situation or how God will fulfil your valid need.

____

____

____

____

____

____

____

____

____

____

____

____

____

____

____

____

____

____

____

____

STEP THREE: ASK GOD FOR INSTRUCTIONS ON HOW TO OVERCOME THE ROOT PROBLEM AND FILL YOUR VALID NEED.

WHAT DID GOD TELL ME TO DO?

Write down the instructions that God gave you.

____

____

____

____

____

____

____

____

____

____

____

____

____

____

____

____

____

____

THE PROCESS TO FREEDOM

Write about your journey as you complete the instructions God gave you.

____

____

____

____

____

____

____

____

____

____

____

____

____

____

____

____

____

____

____

11

NEXT STEP: PUT THIS INTO PRACTICE

Did the book feel like a mirror of where you are right now? If you completed the activities and know you have a lot to process and implement, let us walk with you.

I'd like to invite you to join us in the Pink Flamingo University (PFU) – a training and discipleship community for pink flamingos, like you.

During your first 90 days in PFU, you'll focus on uprooting fear-driven behavioural responses you use to feel peace and comfort, avoid your emotions, and avoid trusting God and others.

After that, you'll continue on a guided path with practical tools, community, and support designed to help you anchor into your God-given identity and develop the emotional and relational maturity to stand as that person without fear.

It's not easy to unlearn years of patterns and ways of being when they're rooted in the fear of being rejected, judged, or abandoned.

Grant us the honour of walking alongside you.

Learn to show up as who God created you to be.

Join your fellow pink flamingos in PFU today and get 10% off your first month.

https://club.findyourpinkflamingo.com/book-readers

NOTES

9. THE ME GOD SEES

1. Moyer, Bill. "Facing Evil." Public Affairs Television, Inc. and KERA/Dallas, Dallas, TX, 1988.

ACKNOWLEDGMENTS

To the Pan Fantasy Steelband in Canada. Thank you for inspiring me as I sat in the back of your practices and grooved to the rhythms of your island beats.
To my grandma, Cynthia Cameron, who believed that Christ would do great things through me even when everyone else thought I was crazy and unprepared to be a Christian.

ABOUT THE AUTHOR

Meet Chañel Robe, founder of the Pink Flamingo University, speaker, trainer, blogger and passionate advocate for being who God created you to be without fear. Having overcome burnout twice and worked to shed her fear-driven self-stifling tendencies, she's now an authority on using a God-focused approach to overcome beliefs and behaviours rooted in the fear of rejection, judgment and abandonment. Chañel now equips others as they ditch their fears and show up as their real selves (what she calls your pink flamingo self) in every single area of life. Her clients have more fulfilling jobs, ministries, marriages, businesses, friendships, etc.

She and her husband, Jeremy, also finance and lead non-profit initiatives designed to heal the psychological wounds of Caribbean slavery.

On a regular day, Chañel enjoys travelling, watching animated movies, and spending time with family, friends, and Jesus.

Please do not hand her pom-poms. She has her own.

Connect with Chañel at
findyourpinkflamingo.com